AMAZING
TALES FROM THE
NEW YORK YANKEES
DUGOUT

A COLLECTION OF THE GREATEST
YANKEES STORIES EVER TOLD

KEN McMILLAN
AND ED RANDALL
WITH BRUCE MARKUSEN

ILLUSTRATIONS BY BOB JACKSON
AND BURKE LaMOTTE

SPORTS
PUBLISHING

Sports Publishing books may be purchased in bulk at special discounts for
sales promotion, corporate gifts, fund-raising, or educational purposes. Special
editions can also be created to specifications. For details, contact the Special Sales
Department, Sports Publishing, 307 West 36th Street, 11th Floor, New York,
NY 10018 or sportspubbooks@skyhorsepublishing.com.

Sports Publishing® is a registered trademark of Skyhorse Publishing, Inc.®, a
Delaware corporation.

Visit our website at www.sportspubbooks.com.

10 9 8 7 6 5 4 3 2

Library of Congress Cataloging-in-Publication Data is available on file.

ISBN: 978-1-61321-024-6

Printed in the United States of America

This book is dedicated to my mother, Rita,
and late father, Wallace.

&

I hope I've made you proud.

—Ken McMillan

&

To Big Ed and Nora for thinking me up and to Gracie, a
living, breathing miracle, for her jaw-dropping, heart-stopping
beauty, elegance, wit, grace, modesty, kindness, adorability,
unwavering support and unconditional love.

&

This book is written in memory of those from September
11 whose spirit shines in the darkness and which most dra-
matically ratified our strength as a people.

The author shares with the world his grief at the loss of so
many innocent lives, our pride in the courage and goodness of
all those assisting the victims and our faith in the triumph of
civilized behavior among all peoples.

Among those, Father Mychal Judge, who I will miss forever, for his wisdom and counsel that completely changed my
attitude about life and love and his unbelievable ability to listen and fill those he listened to with their own dignity and to
tell them that they were truly loved.

—Ed Randall

CONTENTS

ACKNOWLEDGMENTS

Most writers dream of writing books, but very few actually develop an idea and follow it through to its conclusion. In this case, the idea of compiling short stories on the New York Yankees came from The Dreaming Dog Group. I thank the agency for the opportunity to take the idea and run with it. Without The Dog's assistance and faith in a rookie author, this book would not be in your hands. I would also like to thank Mike Pearson of Sports Publishing Inc. for agreeing to publish this book.

I must thank the librarian of my research, faithful Yankees fan Craig Anderson, for supplying me with a seemingly endless supply of resource material on the Yankees.

Valuable technical assistance was provided by Gary Carter and Jeff Ehmann. Without their input my words would have remained locked forever within outdated word processing programs. Their advice and hands-on help moved the project forward at a critical juncture.

Finally, I must thank my many friends and family members who saw to it I kept this project moving in a positive direction. Special thanks goes out to Gary Carter, Diana Kazolias and my mother, Rita McMillan, for their caring and understanding through a painstaking process.

—Ken McMillan

There is no bibliography in this book.*
We therefore acknowledge all those within for their time, graciousness and accessibility, for which I am deeply grateful.

—Ed Randall

*Editorial note: No bibliography appeared in the most recent previous edition of this book, *More Tales from the Yankees Dugout*

JACK AKER

Satchel

Jack Aker became the Yankee closer in 1969 and remained there until 1972, sharing the job with Lindy McDaniel and then being replaced by Sparky Lyle.

Aker came to the majors with the As in Kansas City in 1964. One year later, he became part of a boxscore for the ages. Aker finished the game that Satchel Paige started on September 25, 1965 . . . at the age of 59 years old or possibly a little younger.

Maybe only 57.

Nobody is quite sure.

"I don't know if we were told in advance that Satchel was coming, but I do remember when he walked into the room. At that time, players seemed to know the history of the game more than they do now and everybody, of course, had heard of Satchel Paige. We welcomed him."

Aker remembers Paige saying he would need a few days to get into shape to pitch. Finley planned to start him as a promotion called 'Light A Match for Satch Night.'

"We didn't really know if he was gonna pitch in a game or not but everyday he would come out and throw a little bit on the side. We had no idea how old he was but he had to be probably in his 60s. We watched him throw and he threw alright for a man that age. His control was impeccable. The catchers who warmed him up in the bullpen said they could sit in a rocking chair and catch him."

Speaking of rocking chairs, they brought one into the bullpen for Satchel.

"At that time, we didn't have a very good team so the stands weren't packed. But there was always a group of people who would buy tickets to come sit down by the bullpen to hear Satchel telling stories. He was a very friendly guy who would sit out there and also trade stories with us.

"The Red Sox are coming to town and they have a pretty good hitting club. The As were advertising that Satchel would start against them.

"He took the mound and three innings later he'd given up no runs and one hit. Carl Yastrzemski hit a double off of him to left-centerfield. It was an astounding event. He didn't throw extremely hard. I would guess he could still throw the ball 75 or 80 miles an hour. He threw harder in the game than he had on the sideline but his control was still amazing. He was cruising so easy he could have probably gone more than three innings. And the Red Sox were serious, they didn't let up."

But they did win the game 5-2. Satchel came out after three leading 1-0, giving the one hit and striking out one.

Pepi

"Joe Pepitone was a target of a lot of things that went on. Joe, at that time, had these hairpieces. He had one for off the field and another for on the field. Fans would remember that whenever Joe took off his batting helmet, he very quickly slipped his hat on all in one movement. The helmet came off, the hat went on. He would never be seen without one of these hairpieces. He was also the first guy to ever use a hair dryer in the clubhouse. We all took note of this. Joe would wait and shower by himself usually and then come out with his hairpiece on and proceed to blow-dry it and comb it all down. He was like a woman. He would spend an hour in front of the mirror."

Your attention please, ladies and gentlemen, now pitching for the Yankees, number 19, Fritz Peterson.

"Fritz loaded up Pepi's hair dryer with baby powder one night. At that time, we used to hang around the clubhouse a lot longer than the guys do now. Everybody was sitting around and we had already dressed. We were waiting for Pepi to get out of the shower. When he came out and he turned that hair dryer on, it looked a volcano went through the room. One of the funniest sights I ever saw, his whole upper body was snow white. We had guys rolling on the floor laughing so hard. I don't know if Joe actually was angry, but if it was an act, it was a good act. He was stomping and cussing and throwing things around. A few days later, he was laughing about it."

STAN BAHNSEN

When Baseball Was Baseball

O nce upon a time, pitchers were required to bat in the American League.

When Stan Bahnsen pitched for the Yankees, he was joined in the starting rotation by Mel Stottlemyre, Fritz Peterson and Mike Kekich.

"We had a contest where it was Fritz and I against Mel and Kekich to see which team would get the most hits in a season. This was about 1970. We would have a cutoff date near the end of the season. Wherever we were at the time, the two winners were entertained by the two losers to the finest restaurant in town. It was carte blanche, you could order whatever you wanted, any food, any champagne, anything."

The cutoff date coincided with the Yankees in Cleveland.

"You not only got points for hits, you got a point for hitting a batter.

"Kekich and Stottlemyre edged Fritz and I by a couple of points. They wanted to go to a place called The Kon Tiki which was a Polynesian place that I think was located in the Sheraton. They had all the fancy mai tais and all the exotic drinks and appetizers."

At the same time they were eating and drinking like kings, the winners were being royally screwed.

Stan Bahnsen

"We had to foot the bill but what Stottlemyre didn't know was that we had his American Express card. We got it out of where they keep the valuables in the clubhouse and returned it the next day. They were ordering food they weren't even gonna eat. They've got mai tais, the appetizers, all these drinks with umbrellas in them, extra egg rolls. We're like, 'That's fine, that's fine. You guys won.' They were trying to get our goat. What they didn't know was Stottlemyre was paying for this whole thing. Fritz and I staged this argument when the bill came, 'I'll get it, no, I'll get it.'"

After the season, the United States Postal Service delivered the latest American Express bill to the Stottlemyre residence.

"I remember that about a month after the season, Fritz and I got phone calls from Mel. He was really hot. His wife saw the bill and she says, 'What was this?'"

They did end up paying Stottlemyre back.

"He never missed the card because he wasn't paying for anything that night. But he did pay for everything that night."

Is That Who I Think It Is?

Fritz Peterson developed a reputation as an instigator of practical jokes. But this was Stan Bahnsen at his best.

"Mike Kekich had bought a waterbed. They had just come out in the late 60s, early 70s. We are on a nine- or 10-day road trip and he had bought one in Chicago. It was in a box that was about 20 inches square. I asked him what was in the box. He said, 'I just got a waterbed.' I said, 'We'll probably use an ice pick to punch some holes in it before the roadtrip is over.'"

Soon, the waterbed was nowhere to be found.

"Nobody could figure out where it was. I don't know how he hid it. We figured he must have shipped it back because he was worried about sabotage."

The last game of the long road trip was in Milwaukee.

"I come into the clubhouse and my locker was by Kekich's. I saw a box under some towels and it was the damn waterbed. I wasn't gonna poke holes in it, but I wanted to play a trick on him."

Let the chicanery begin.

"At County Stadium, the top of the scoreboard had an automobile on top of it. If anybody hit for the cycle, they win this car. It's up there on a platform. It must have been lifted up there with a crane. I gave the clubhouse kid 10 bucks and told him I wanted him to drape this waterbed over the top of the car. And he did it."

Batting practice is over and the pitchers are running together in the outfield.

"I made it a point to be by Kekich because I wanted to get him to look at the scoreboard because he never would. Every time we would run a sprint, I would look back. Finally, he says, 'What do you keep looking at?' I said, 'I'm just trying to check the out-of-town scores.' After a while, he says, 'What game are you looking at?' I said, 'The Baltimore game.' That was at the top of the scoreboard.

And then Mike Kekich turned around and saw his waterbed.

"This was about 20-30 minutes before game time. He sees this black thing draped over this compact car. He went crazy. He quit running with me and went into the clubhouse to get his game uniform on. Then I saw him running out toward center field."

To get to the platform atop the scoreboard, there was a catwalk that was straight up about 75 feet, a very intimidating presence.

"He went all the way up this ladder to this trap door. But there was a lock on it. He had to come all the way back down the ladder and had to go find someone who had a key for this lock. He finally found someone who had the key."

The timing couldn't have been any better.

"They just started to play the national anthem. The flag-pole is right next to the scoreboard. They're playing, 'Oh say, can you see' and this trap door opens and here comes Kekich up on top of the scoreboard in his #18 Yankee uniform and he's pulling his waterbed off the top of that car. It was so funny."

Kekich accused Bahnsen of planting the waterbed on the scoreboard. Bahnsen vigorously denied it. As payback, before the flight back to New York, Kekich got hold of some luggage tags and placed them on Bahnsen's bags.

They read "Honolulu."

That's A Lock

The Yankees had just lost a doubleheader in Chicago on getaway day.

"Fritz got into this lock thing. He would get bicycle padlocks and lock stuff up. I had these shoes with buckles on them and Fritz locked them together. I had to be on the bus in five minutes. I'm sitting in my locker and I'm so mad. I know who did it. I'm like screw it, I'm not going to LA."

As the manager, Ralph Houk is the last guy to leave for the bus. He sees Bahnsen and asks the obvious question.

"He says, 'Bahnsen, what's goin' on?' I say, 'I can't go.' He says, 'Why can't you go?' I say, 'I can't put my shoes on.' He was not in a very good mood. He says, 'Why can't you?' I say, 'Because they're locked together.' He says, 'Well, somebody better get you a goddamn key because if you don't make that bus, you're gonna get fined.' Somehow they got a key and I made the bus by about a minute."

STEVE BALBONI

Waiting a Lifetime

S teve Balboni will never forget his first major league at-bat. "It was pretty intimidating. That 1981 team was almost like an All-Star team. It was a great team to be part of."

Balboni was getting advanced billing. He had heard that Phil Rizzuto and Frank Messer were building him up, talking about him on radio and TV while he was still in the minor leagues.

"I don't remember how many people were there. It seemed like a million. There was a good crowd there and it seemed incredibly loud.

"I remember walking up to the plate and it was so loud, I couldn't believe it. On every pitch, it seemed to get louder."

Balboni faced fellow rookie Howard Bailey of Detroit and all 6-3, 225 pounds of him hit a triple. With that blinding speed?

"With that big ballpark. I hit it about 425 feet and it didn't go out."

I Wanna Be a Part of It,
New York, New York

Steve Balboni would have loved to have played his entire career in New York.

"I had a great experience, too, in Kansas City. We won a World Series there and the people there were excellent. We lived there for eight years. Even though I knew it was gonna be tougher to break into the line-up with the Yankees and I was going to Kansas City to play every day, it was tough. I still had mixed feelings when I got traded."

You never forget the ghosts.

"I enjoyed being part of that tradition, the way they go about things. Watching them on TV the last few years, watching the way they play, it's like this is what it's all about. I've seen other teams and been on other teams where it's just not the same. It's almost like it's an effort for people to go out there. Guys really don't care as much. I played in Seattle before they sold the team and things were turned around there. It was unbelievable. We lost like nine games in a row and nobody seemed to care from the front office down."

Based on that experience, Balboni says there is no place like New York.

"I don't think there is any team like New York. Winning is important. That's what makes it more fun and that's the way I felt about baseball."

How about this for an epilogue?

"The one thing I liked was nobody was bigger than the pinstripes. Everybody had the same goal and if you weren't for the team, you weren't there very long."

HANK BAUER

War is Hell

As we continue to engage in a war different than any other this country has ever waged, no Yankee, past or present, can appreciate it more than Hank Bauer.

One of nine children, he was a child of the Depression. When the Japanese attacked Pearl Harbor, the most unprecedented surprise attack this country experienced until September 11, Bauer enlisted in the Marine Corps.

He was assigned to the Pacific theater and grew into manhood in hells called Guadalcanal, Guam and Okinawa, where his men captured the airfield at considerable cost.

Hank Bauer was one of only six of 64 soldiers who survived the fierce battle. He suffered a shrapnel injury, remnants of which he would play with for the duration of his baseball career.

In his four years of service to our country, Hank Bauer was awarded two Purple Hearts and two bronze stars.

Hank Bauer holds the record for the longest hitting streak in the World Series, 17 games. His Yankees won seven championships in nine years before he was dealt to Kansas City near the end of his career in the deal for Roger Maris.

Having seen hell on Earth, he could identify with another flag-raising: by New York City firefighters at Ground Zero, days after the terrorist attack.

One Subjective Theory

One of Hank Bauer's eight siblings, a brother 3 1/2 years his senior named Herman, "was a better ballplayer than I was."

And he never let Yogi Berra forget it.

"I told Yogi one time, 'You know, Yog, you wouldn't have made a pimple on my brother's ass as a catcher. But you're a hell of a lot better hitter.'"

Herman Bauer never fulfilled his promise as a player. He died at The Battle of Normandy.

Of All the Places to Get Hit

During World War II, Hank Bauer won not one Purple Heart but two.

"I got one on Guam and one in Okinawa. The one on Okinawa was the worst one. I got hit in the left thigh.

"One day we're playing in Yankee Stadium and I think it was Tom Gorman was pitching against us."

Guess where he hit Hank Bauer?

"He hit me right where that damn shrapnel went in and it was stinging. So I got to first base and put my hand on it. Hell, I had a big lump there and I called time. I ran into the dugout and called over our trainer, Gus Mauch. I pulled my pants down and there was a big blood clot there. Casey saw it and said, "Get him the hell out of here. Take him in the training room." Gus put ice on it and it went away right away. It really stung."

Bauer went on the disabled list. Just kidding.

Hank turns 80 in July. "I told my doctor 'I owe my longevity to scotch and cigarettes.' That didn't go over too good."

DAVE BERGMAN

A Deceiving O-Fer

I n his first call-up to the show at the end of the 1975 season after winning the Double-A Eastern League batting title, Dave Bergman went 0-for-17. He only struck out four times.

"I have to tell you, between you, me and the fence-post, I certainly didn't swing the bat all that well. But there were about four particular plays, two on bunts and two that were hit up the middle that I, in my own mind, thought not only I was safe, I was safe by at least a step."

Back in those days, unless it was a clean hit, a rookie was banged out.

"I was a little disenchanted with the results. However, in retrospect, it was a great learning experience. I thought I could have just as easily been 4-for-17 or even 5-for-17."

His last game was against Jim Palmer.

"I went 0-for-4 but hit the ball right on the screws twice. Of the 17 at-bats, I felt like I had eight good at-bats and nine terrible at-bats."

Preparing for the Future

Dave Bergman was one of those rare players who did not embark upon his professional career until he graduated from college. In this case, from Illinois State University armed with a business administration degree and a focus in finance. Seventeen seasons and 1,349 games and one great pension later, he entered the business arena managing other players money. *While* he was playing, not after.

"I went to school and worked every off-season. I'm a firm believer that athletes, if they're gonna waste their time, they need to waste their time in the off-season trying to figure out what they want to do when their career is over. The reason is that most athletes, after their career is over, spend five, six, seven years floundering, trying to find a profession that is acclimated for their intelligence, or something they really like to do."

Bergman had a different theory when it came to himself.

"I felt 'why don't I do that while I'm playing and when I'm done, I'm ready to roll n' roll in the field I know I want to pursue.'"

Bergman's potential clients were right there in the locker room with him.

"My first professional client was Alan Trammell. At that time, I was helping him invest his money. I was not personally investing his money. He had somebody else doing it. When I retired, he called me and said he wanted to be my first professional client."

Bergman prides himself in knowing the field, actually, two of them, baseball and business.

"One of the things that helps me in the business that I'm in is these guys can't trick me. I know all their tricks. I know when they sleep, I know when they eat, I know how they think. In many cases, I can think five years ahead for them because I know some of the issues that are gonna take place in their professional career."

Which makes him invaluable.

YOGI BERRA

Listen To These!

Yogi Berra's fame was born out of 14 World Series appearances with the Yankees (which included 10 titles) and 15 consecutive All-Star Games.

His legend grew with his familiar malapropisms, known as "Yogi-isms." A sampling:

- "It ain't over till it's over."
- "It's deja vu all over again."
- Speaking of two nights held in his honor in New York and his hometown of St. Louis: "I want to thank all of the people for making this night possible."
- Asked what time it was, he said, "You mean now?"
- "A nickel ain't worth a dime anymore."
- "Baseball is 90 percent mental. The other half is physical."
- "If the people don't want to come out to the ballpark, nobody's going to stop them."
- During spring training a trainer asked Berra what hat size he required. His reply: "I don't know. I'm not in shape yet."
- Speaking of a restaurant, he said, "Nobody goes there anymore. It's too crowded."
- "I usually take a two-hour nap, from one to four."

Yogi Berra

- "I'd rather be the Yankees catcher than the president, and that makes me pretty lucky, I guess, because I could never be the president."
- "I've been with the Yankees for 17 years watching games and learning. You can see a lot by observing."
- Mary Lindsay, the wife of New York City major John Lindsay, once commented how Berra appeared nice and cool one day, to which Berra replied, "You don't look so hot yourself."
- Johnny Bench received a telegram from Berra after the Cincinnati Reds star broke the Yankee's all-time home run record for catchers. It read: "Congratulations on breaking my record. I always thought it would stand until it was broken."
- "If you come to a fork in the road, take it."

Outfielder Charley Keller spoke fondly of Berra and his Yogi-isms. "He had a way of saying things that made you think and smile and then say, 'I would never say it that way, but I know what he means.' Sometimes it seemed to make more sense the way he said it than the regular way, and that may have been a part of his charm."

Quote, End Quote

"What you have to do when you consider Yogi is think about where he started and where he ended. I don't mean that he was poor—a lot of us were that. I mean that all he ever wanted to be was a baseball player, and almost everyone told him he couldn't be one. He not only became a ballplayer, he became a great one and one of the most loved and respected of the last 50 years. Every time I see him I feel good."

—Former teammate Jerry Coleman

You Need To Know This

How did Lawrence Peter Berra earn the nickname "Yogi?"

His friends had seen a Hindu fakir in a movie sitting still with arms and legs folded. It reminded them of Berra as he sat between innings.

The Master Motivator

Yogi Berra had a very competitive drive as a player, and he would try any method to get one of his pitchers to perform better.

With Vic Raschi, Berra used to insult him, calling him "Onion Head," or challenging his performance.

"Is that as hard as you can throw it?" Berra would ask Raschi if a fastball didn't live up to the catcher's expectations.

Berra was also a chatterbox behind the plate, trying to find a mental edge by getting into a player's head as he stood in the batter's box.

Sometimes it was more than words that came out of Berra's mouth.

"I knew that when the hitter said, 'Yogi, shut up,' I was going good," Berra said.

Ken "Hawk" Harrelson recalls his rookie season with Kansas City and how his game with the Yankees was being televised by NBC. Down 0-2 in the count, Harrelson was still thinking about his mom watching on television back in Georgia when he felt something warm on the back of his sock. By time he realized what had happened, Whitey Ford blew strike three past him.

"Yogi had spit on my calf just before Whitey delivered," Harrelson said. "I was dumbfounded. As I turned, my mouth hanging open, I am sure, Yogi said, 'welcome to the big leagues, kid.'"

A Thriller

"In some ways wearing a Yankee uniform for 25 years was the biggest thrill I ever had. . . . Putting on the pinstripes was the best thing that ever happened to me. . . . Being a Yankee was all it was cracked up to be and then some."

—Yogi Berra

Discipline

Known as a free swinger at the plate, manager Bucky Harris wanted Berra to show more patience. So Berra—who was once told by Boston Red Sox great hitter Ted Williams that he was "an awful sight" at the plate and gave hitting "a bad name"—went up to the plate and took three pitches for strikes.

When Harris demanded to know what he was doing up there, Berra shot back, "It's your fault. How do you expect a guy to hit and think, to think and hit at the same time?"

Of course, Williams also heaped great praise on Berra's ability to hit in the clutch.

"He looked like hell, but what happened when he attacked the ball was right out of a computer. He could move the runner, and move him late in the game like no one else I ever saw play the game."

He's No House Boy

Bobby Richardson was asked to stay with Berra and his wife in his New Jersey home.

Pulling up to the expansive manse, Richardson asked Berra how many rooms there were.

Said Yogi: "I don't know. Carmen takes care of that."

Temperature Check

Trainer Dennis Liborio was watching Berra gingerly step into a whirlpool and then watching the catcher sort of jump up and down without saying anything.

He asked Berra if the water was too hot.

"How hot is it supposed to be?" Berra asked.

Gracious Close

"Baseball is a great way to spend your life if you are successful, and I was. Going to a game with your family is also a great thing to do. It can make you understand your kids, and they can get to know you. All those good things. It is a wonderful thing for you to do in the afternoon, at night, and from April until October. All summer. You can start when the first robin builds a nest and see baseball until the geese fly south."

—Yogi Berra on baseball

JOHNNY BLANCHARD

You Want Anchovies With That?

I t's 1955 and Johnny Blanchard has just completed his Eastern League season in Binghamton, New York, where he won the home run and RBI crowns. He was heading home, or so he thought.

"The last game of the season, the wife and I had packed up the car and we were all ready to drive back to Minnesota. After the last game, the whole club went up to a little pizza parlor for some pizza and a couple of beers."

About midnight, the phone rang in the pizza parlor. The caller asked for Johnny Blanchard.

"Some guy's on the line saying he's George Weiss. I didn't know it. He says, 'Blanch, we want you to report tomorrow morning to Yankee Stadium. Well I told the guy, 'Yeah, yeah. Have another beer, pal,' and I hung up the phone."

Blanchard started back to the table and the phone rang again. Of course, it was for him.

"The guy said to me, 'Don't you hang up again. This is George Weiss. You be here tomorrow by noon.' And it was really George Weiss."

The Blanchards drove all night to the Bronx, "an adventure and a half," and checked into the hotel at 10 a.m. He was at the Stadium at noon.

It's Not Just a Job, It's An Adventure

When he wasn't spelling Yogi Berra or Elston Howard behind the plate, Johnny Blanchard found playing time in the outfield.

"We were playing a ballgame in 1961 one evening in Cleveland and Houk put me in right field. Of course, I was no gazelle out there. Bobby Richardson was playing second base.

"In the old Cleveland ballpark, there was an opening in the stands through which the sun would shine. At about 8 or 8:10 at night, it would hit the right-fielder dead in his eyes, just above the hitter."

Blanchard would put the bill of his cap down and his hand up to block the sun. But he was also blocking the hitter out.

"For about eight minutes there was no way until that sun dips down that you can see."

It's eight minutes of hell.

"Especially for a guy like me. I was no Mickey Mantle in the outfield, I was no Hank Bauer by any means."

Willie Kirkland, the Indians outfielder, stepped to the plate. You know what's coming next.

"I saw him take a swing. I know he swung at the ball by his feet, by his legs and all. But I didn't have a clue where the ball went. Right away, I looked at Richardson at second base. Bobby kept pointing to the foul line. I kept drifting over toward the area of the pole. I looked back at him and he kept pointing like it was a foul ball."

Blanchard is looking up trying to pick the ball up and starts banging his glove.

"I get over to the stands and the people are howling. One guy yells out at me, 'Hey, dummy, the ball is in right-center out of the park.' I looked down at Bobby and he was facing me and had his hands on his knees. I could see his shoulders were just jiggling he was laughing so hard he couldn't pick his head up. As soon as the ball was hit, Bobby knew it was out of the park. I'm in the corner dancing around, looking for the ball, just hoping it doesn't hit me in the head."

"Richardson says, 'Blanch, I had to give it to you. I know you didn't see it. I knew it was gone.'"

That's the last time Johnny Blanchard took direction from Bobby Richardson.

JIM BOUTON

Hats Off

Because baseball is all about statistical overload, somebody actually counted the number of times Jim Bouton's hat flew off his head during his World Series victory over the Cardinals in Game Three of the 1964 World Series.

The answer is 47.

"The hat came off because of my pitching motion. I used the trunk of my body to get a lot of my velocity. This means that the top part of my body would propel forward so I would use my legs, my arm and the forward motion of my body and I used the top part of my body more than most pitchers. Because of that snapping action, my hat would pop off my head. I had problems with that in the minors. It was nothing that just started happening at Yankee Stadium."

This started when Bouton started throwing the ball hard.

"Toward the end of my last year in the minor leagues, my 1961 season when I was pitching in the Texas League for Amarillo, my hat would start coming off my head. That's when my velocity got up pretty high."

Bouton doesn't know how hard he was throwing because they didn't have radar guns in those days.

"I would estimate it probably somewhere about 105 to 110 miles an hour."

A Fish Story A.K.A. It Sounds Fishy to Me

During spring training in 1963, on the morning after a night game, it was time for Mickey Mantle's fishing contest in the canals of Fort Lauderdale.

"You would go there with your roommate, leave the dock at 8 a.m. and come back at noon. Everybody would put 20 bucks or something like that and at the end, the boat that caught the most fish would spilt the pot with the boat that caught the biggest fish."

Bouton says that he and his roommate, the legendary Phil Linz, were terrible fishermen.

"Linz and I are driving along this highway in Florida about seven o'clock in the morning and we see a bait & tackle store along the side of the road. There was a freezer out in front of the place."

Bouton told Linz to pull in. He had a hunch.

"I was gonna buy a fish, but the place was closed. But I happened to open the freezer and there was this gigantic fish inside, probably something from the sea. It was huge, probably about 25 pounds, a monster fish. It might have been a bass or tuna. I see this guy and I say, 'How much do you want for this fish?' He says, 'Oh, you can have it. That's been in there for three years. You can't eat it.' I say, 'That's OK, we don't need to eat it.'

Bouton and Linz left with the fish and put it in the bottom of the cooler that had beer and sandwiches in it and covered it with ice.

"We get out to our boat, get out around the corner, took the fish out of the cooler, attached a line to it and dunked him in the water. Our only hope was that he would thaw out by the time we came back to the dock. It was frozen stiff, solid as a rock. Everyone once in a while, we would lift him out of the water and put a little sun on him to see how he was thawing out."

Now they're playing pretend.

"We're out there fishing and of course, we're not catching a damn thing."

Jim Bouton

They don't have to. They have the thing won.

"We know we have the winner. We know we have the biggest fish and we may even also win for poundage. We know we're in pretty good shape."

That's when Tom Tresh and Joe Pepitone drove by.

"Hey, how you guys doing?" We say, 'We caught a couple.' They say, 'Let's see what you got.' We said, 'Well, we're only gonna show you part of it.' We lifted it about a third of the way up and they said some bad words."

Bouton and Linz made sure they were the last ones back to the dock so that they could make a grand entrance.

"We pull up to the dock and there the players are with fish all spread out. Whitey and Mickey have about 15 fish, Boyer and Stafford have about eight fish of decent size, a couple of nice five- or six-pounders in there."

And now it is showtime.

"We haul our fish off the boat and lay him down next to all these other fish. It looked like our guy could have eaten all the rest of them for lunch and have plenty of room left over. They weighed it and it was something like 22 pounds."

Bouton and Linz were awarded half the money for cheating. But that's not the end of the story.

"Sometime later, Mickey came over to me and said, 'I've been thinking about that fish. How come ours were green and flipping around and yours was gray and just lying there?' I said, 'We caught him first thing in the morning and we were dragging him around all day.'"

Accentuate The Positive

Managers sometimes have to coax their players through their troubles, whether they be physical or emotional.

Jim Bouton

The power of positive persuasion is something Johnny Keane used to his advantage.

Mickey Mantle recalled a conversation that went as follows:

"How do your legs feel today, Mick?"

"Not too good," Mantle replied.

"Yes, but how do they feel?"

"It hurts when I run, the right one especially. I can't stride on it or anything."

"Well, do you think you can play?" Keane would ask.

"I don't know. I guess I can play. Yeah, hell, what the hell. Sure I can play," Mantle said, giving in.

"Good. Great. We need you out there. Unless you're hurt—unless it really hurts you. I don't want you to play if you're hurt."

"No, it's okay. I hurt, but it's okay. I'll watch it."

"Good, good. We sure need you."

Mantle's teammates would get a kick out of this. Jim Bouton would play the role of Keane when he'd ask Mantle, "Mick, how does your leg feel?"

"Well, it's severed at the knee," Mantle would deadpan.

"Yes, but does it hurt?"

"No, I scotch-taped it back into place."

"And how's your back?"

"My back is broken in seven places."

"Can you swing the bat?"

"Yeah, I can swing. If I can find some more scotch tape."

"Great. Well, get in there then. We need you."

*   *   *   *

Struggling pitchers will listen to just about anyone to cure their ills.

Jim Bouton was in such a sorry state he actually listened to some tips offered by restaurant owner Toots Shor.

"Once when I was going bad," Bouton said, "he told me my whole problem was that I was striding three inches too far and if I just shortened up on the stride by those three inches everything would be fine. I was so desperate I actually tried it." He added, "It didn't help."

Just How Close?

How close was Jim Bouton to becoming a one-game major leaguer?

Inches.

In his first Yankee Stadium start as a rookie in 1962, Bouton opened with eight pitches out of the strike zone. With the count at 3-1 on the third Washington Senators hitter, Bouton threw another ball. Or so he thought, as did manager Ralph Houk, who was stepping out of the dugout. Turns out, the home plate umpire called a strike. Bouton survived not only the first inning but the entire game.

He shut out the Senators on seven hits and seven walks. Left fielder Hector Lopez bailed Bouton out with four leaping catches.

Following the game, Bouton walked back into the locker room just in time to see Mickey Mantle laying down the final white towel, completing a carpet to the victor's locker.

"I'll never forget him for that," Bouton said.

Ol' No. 56, And Don't Forget It!

Jim Bouton was handed uniform number 56 during spring training in 1962. When it appeared he was going to make the team, clubhouse manager Pete Sheehy said he could give Bouton number 27 to wear.

"I told him I'd keep 56 because I wanted it to remind me of how close I was to not making the club."

The Doc

Ever hear this Henny Youngman joke?

Guy goes into a doctor's office, sticks his arm out and says, "Doctor, doctor. It hurts when I do this."

"Well, don't do that," the doctor replied.

That's the way some Yankees felt about visiting Dr. Sidney Gaynor.

Jim Bouton broke the thumb on his pitching hand while toiling in the minors in Auburn, New York. The good doc removed the cast from Bouton's hand, examined it closely and told him he had a broken thumb and that he shouldn't bump it into anything.

A couple years later, Bouton went for another checkup. Gaynor put Bouton through some stretching exercises and then told him, "You got a sore arm."

"Yeah, I know. It hurts when I throw."

Gaynor scowled at Bouton and offered, "If it's sore, don't throw."

"How long?" Bouton inquired. "I don't know," Gaynor said. "When it starts feeling better then you can start throwing again."

CLETIS BOYER

Learning From the Master

In 1994, Derek Jeter of the Columbus Clippers was named the Minor League Player of the Year. Problem was he was experiencing fielding problems, specifically, throwing problems. He made a staggering 54 errors.

Flip ahead to spring training, 1995, replacement player spring training. Enter one of the best ever to put an infielder's glove on, Cletis Boyer, coaching in spring training.

"I'm watching Derek work out. Every ground ball hit to him, he was looking the ball into his glove and his glove, most of the time, was going through his legs. Then he would come up and throw."

Boyer told Jeter that he must have made an error and somebody told him to look the ball into his glove. Jeter said that was the case.

"For a year and a half, he was following the ball into his glove. Somebody told me he was throwing a lot of balls up into the seats. He made 25 or 30 errors throwing."

Boyer said "we had about six instructors in the organization teaching that didn't know how to teach. We had six instructors that never had one day of pro ball. So how the hell could you teach a kid how to play?"

Boyer said to Jeter, "I'm gonna ask you a question and I'm not gonna trick you. Where are you trying to throw to the first baseman, what area? He said, 'Chest high.' I said, 'Oh. With your arm, you're gonna throw chest high? If you leave the ball up a tiny bit, it's your error.'"

Boyer knew about first base play. As an active player, he used to take grounders there. He then imparted his wisdom.

"I want you to throw the ball to my waist. But if you miss me, miss me low or miss me in. I can actually catch it on the ground and I can tag him in."

In five weeks taking throws at first, Derek Jeter never pulled Clete Boyer off of first down the right field line. He threw three balls over his head that he didn't have to jump for.

Boyer told him, "Just try to keep low. If the ball is hit at you, just try to have your glove on the ground first," which he does.

Clete Boyer says everyone in the organization wanted to move Derek Jeter to the outfield. Meanwhile, he was making this bold assertion.

"Honest to God, I said before he ever played in the big leagues that he was gonna be the greatest Yankee shortstop ever. He is. You can see it. He could have been in the big leagues the next week. That's all he needed."

Think about the tutor every time you see Derek Jeter field a ball.

Degrees of Separation

Clete Boyer, Carney Lansford, Wade Boggs, Scott Brosius. Boyer had a profound effect on them all, transforming each into Gold Glove-caliber third basemen. The tutorials started when Boyer and Lansford were with Oakland.

"I said I'm gonna talk to you in spring training about infield. Carney was the most serious guy I've ever seen. He was like Mattingly. He was unbelievable. He came to spring training. I got him down and open and stretching with those hamstrings.

You gotta be like a rubber band. He told me later he had to crawl up and down the stairs because his hamstrings were so tight. People don't stretch their hamstrings out. In other words, you can't get down low."

Years later in Oakland, Lansford taught Brosius how to play the way Boyer years prior taught him.

"I'll tell you the biggest thrill I had in spring training last year. It was talking to Scott Brosius. I loved that guy. You see how he plays? He said to me, 'Are you the guy who taught Carney Lansford how to play third?' I said, 'Yeah.'"

Boyer had just one question for Brosius.

"When you charge the ball that you have to bare-hand and throw on the run, I want to know where you're trying to throw the ball. He said, 'I have to throw the ball five or six feet on the inside of first.' A lot of people make that play but hit the runner or throw it away because of your momentum going in. The three years I was there, I never saw him screw that play up."

While Brosius was in Oakland, Boggs was winning his first Gold Glove with the Yankees.

"Honest to God, Boggs will tell you, I never talked to him in front of anybody. I never told him he had to do this. When he came to us, he was a stand-up third baseman. And when your feet are close together, you can't go to your right and you can't dive to you right."

Oh, you can dive.

"You can dive, but the ball is 30 feet by you by the time you hit the ground.

"Chipper Jones is the worst right now. His hands are up above his knees. So how's he gonna catch balls down the line? He has to move his right foot first for his left foot to cross over. He can't do it."

RALPH BRANCA

Who Knew?

Ralph Branca, the personification of the Brooklyn Dodgers, moved on Detroit where he pitched with a bad hose. That would explain his release during the '54 season, returning to his native Mt. Vernon and taking matters into his own hands.

"The Tigers' general manager was one of those know-it-alls who never talked to the trainer. After I got released, I came home and started throwing at the local field. The Yankees, at the time, were on the road. When they got home, I picked up the phone and called Casey and asked if I could work out. I thought I still could pitch.

"I'm warming up on the sideline near home plate to throw batting practice and Jim Turner, the pitching coach, looks at me and he said, 'Hey, you didn't throw like that at Detroit.' I said, 'No, I was pitching with a sore arm.' That was always one of my faults, I always wanted the ball. Other guys had sore arms and they didn't pitch but I kept pitching. It ended up that the Yankees signed me."

Ralph said it wasn't weird donning pinstripes.

"I played against the Yankees and knew many of them. I was friendly with Whitey and Yogi, knew Mickey, and Lopat became a good friend. I really wasn't a total stranger."

So why did he pick up the phone and call the Yankees and not the Dodgers?

"Well, I guess they were home."

Branca didn't pitch a whole lot for a Yankee club that won 103 games and went home, losing out to the 111-win Cleveland Indians.

"I started in Baltimore and threw a knee-high pitch and the umpire wouldn't give it to me and I wasn't smart enough to raise my sights two inches. The strike zone in the National League was the knee and in the American League from the top of the knee and this guy called it that way. The National League was a low-ball league and the American League was a high-ball league. I can remember Rizzuto yelling at the ump from shortstop, 'Where are those pitches?'

"I probably walked about four or five guys and only pitched about four innings. But they only got one run off me.

"Then my next start was on Old Timers Day against the Red Sox and I went seven innings. The score was 1 to 1 and Moose Skowron got a basehit with men on pinch-hitting for me and the Yankees won the game and I won the game 3 to 1."

But disappointment was warming up in the bullpen.

"The next week I went up to Boston and figured I would pitch again. I had only given up three or four hits but I didn't pitch. They put me in the bullpen. I gave up a run, but the Yankees got a couple of runs. I would have been the winning pitcher but whoever came in didn't hold the lead. And I don't think I pitched after that."

Ralph Branca had a bonus coming if he stayed with them. They didn't want to pay that bonus so they released him after the season. He then signed with the New York Giants' top farm club in Minneapolis.

"Some people still come up to me and remember me with the Yankees. They saw my picture somewhere in a Yankee uniform. Number 24."

BOBBY BROWN

Dr. Bobby Brown, Noted Cardiologist, That Story is True

The idea that Bobby Brown would be a roommate of Yogi Berra's is a perfectly reasonable notion. The idea that one would be reading medical books while the other was reading comic books sounds apocryphal.

"I had to take some exams when I got back to school following the 1946 season, my rookie year. I had to take pathology and pharmacology exams. I had completed the courses except for two weeks and they were long courses. They took almost three-fourths of our school year so they were big exams. I took my pathology book on the road and would I would study it during the day when we weren't playing."

His roommate was not studying pathology.

"Yogi would read comic books. They were 10 cents apiece in those days. He'd buy a dollar's worth. One night, we both finished about the same time. I closed my book and he closed his comic book, looked at me and said, "So how did yours come out?"

Lucky 7

In 41 postseason at-bats, Bobby Brown had an astounding .707 slugging percentage.

"I had 18 hits and nine of them for extra-bases."

It's as if playing in the Series was nothing special.

"It was just one of those things were things happened to work out. I can't tell you why. I always thought it was because I was hidden in that line-up. We had so damn many good hitters that they breathed a sigh of relief when they saw me coming up."

Brown used to hit sixth. In one Series against Brooklyn, he hit fifth.

"I was hitting behind Yogi and DiMaggio and those guys. I sneaked by and didn't embarrass myself anyway."

Yogi

Bobby Brown first met Yogi as minor leaguers with the Yankees' Newark farm club, a team that, at first, did not take him seriously.

"I guess about 10 days after the season started, we were in Rochester on our first road-trip. We heard that we were gonna get a pitcher named Monk Dubiel who was coming down from the Yankees. He reported and along with him was this little guy and no one knew who he was. Dubiel said the Yankees had told him to bring him along.

"I said, 'What's his name?' He said, 'His name is Yogi.'

"He didn't even know his last name.

"Nobody could believe he was a player. When he came into the clubhouse, the trainer looked at him and wouldn't give him a locker. He said, 'Just hang your clothes on the nail over there.' Yogi said, 'I'm a player. I have a contract to play with this team.'"

The manager was no refuge either.

"George Selkirk was the manager and he looked at him. You know how he looked in a uniform. So Selkirk says, 'Listen, we only get 30 minutes to hit on the road. I don't want you to take up the time of the regulars hitting. You just kind of shag balls in the outfield till we get to Newark and then we'll work you out.' They wouldn't even let him hit."

The first day of the homestand in Newark, Selkirk had Yogi at the park for his 2 p.m. audition.

"We had a night game that night and I went out there at five o'clock.

"Selkirk was sitting there in the clubhouse kind of staring off into space. I said, 'George, how did Yogi do?' He said, 'He hit them over the light towers.' That's when he started playing and never sat down again."

Looks can be deceiving.

Johnny Callison

"I had such a hard time with the Cubs, but it was a surprise to come to the Yankees. I was happy to go over there because Ralph Houk was such a helluva guy and I enjoyed playing for him. He made me feel comfortable."

Callison said that first year was scary.

"I come from Bakersfield, a little town in California. You always hear about Yankee Stadium. It overwhelms you. But then you get on the field and it's another ballfield. But it's impressive."

Callison and his family never moved to New York, remaining in the Philadelphia area where he had made a name for himself years before.

"I live right off the Turnpike here and I commuted back and forth because I wasn't playing every day. You're close enough and yet you're not close enough. I didn't want to live in New York, I knew that."

Callison says the commute was tough.

"It was 100 miles door-to-door. I had my GTO running up and down that Turnpike. I could make it in an hour and a half at night, an hour, forty minutes daytime. I only got two tickets. That Turnpike, they sneak up on you."

Drive it every day and you get to know where the speed traps are.

"I figured that out after I got a couple of tickets."

The Yellow Rose of the Bronx?

Johnny Callison's most famous swing came in New York City, across town at Shea Stadium when his three-run home run in the bottom of the ninth off Dick Radatz won the 1964 All-Star Game for the National League. But something that happened to him as a Yankee touched him even more.

"In '72, we had a pretty decent team. We were right in it until the last week or so. CBS owned the club then. I'll never forget, one night I hit a double to knock in the winning run and they sent my wife a dozen yellow roses, which I never heard of. That impressed the hell out of me. Of course, Steinbrenner got there and he got rid of all us old guys."

RICK CERONE

A Real-Life 99-pound Weakling

"I wrestled my freshman year at Essex Catholic High School in New Jersey. I was five feet tall and 99 pounds. My father said eventually I was gonna grow, wrestling is a tough sport and said maybe I should find something else. My best friend is growing up came from a fencing family. So we played football, baseball and we fenced. I got into fencing, enjoyed it and became a state champion in New Jersey. One of my teammates was Peter Westbrook, who fenced in the Olympics. I actually did a little bit in college at Seton Hall as well. All because I was a five-foot, 99-pound weakling as a freshman in high school."

Bad Reception

After high school, Rick Cerone received a tryout from the Yankees which was held at the Stadium in the summer of 1972.

"I was playing American Legion ball and we had played a night game the night before. I went back down to the Jersey shore to a summer house that all the Cerones went

Rick Cerone

to. At about 9 o'clock in the morning, we got a phone call from a local scout saying, 'Rick, if you want, there's a tryout for the Yankees but you have to be at the Stadium by 11 o'clock.'"

On this day, Rick's father was off from work.

"He said, 'Let's go.' And then we realized we had no uniform. The only uniform we had was my Legion uniform that was being washed. So we had to take it out of the washing machine."

Now picture this.

"On the way up the Garden State Parkway trying to dry it out, we had it hanging on the antenna of the car. People were looking at it. There was a jock, there's the underwear, there's the uniform. They thought we were crazy. To be honest with you, over that hour drive up to Yankee Stadium, the uniform did not completely dry. So when I got there, I was all excited. There were about 250 high school players and some college players. But I guarantee you I was the only one in a wet, wet uniform."

But it was clean.

CHRIS CHAMBLISS

Welcome to New York

It was a shock when the Yankees broke up a clique when they traded four pitchers to Cleveland in April, 1974 for Chris Chambliss, Dick Tidrow and Cecil Upshaw.

It was also jarring to Chambliss who was going the other way. He had inadvertently gone out in a blaze of glory.

"We were home playing the Angels and had the bases loaded in the eighth inning against Nolan Ryan. I think we were down by about two runs. I hit a line-drive down the leftfield line that cleared the bases. It was exciting because it put us ahead. We played one more inning and we won. We're in the clubhouse and everybody's jumping up and down because it celebration time."

And then it suddenly got quiet.

"Ken Aspromonte, who was also my Triple-A manager, was our manager. He had replaced Alvin Dark. He called me into the office. He really liked me a lot but he had a sad look on his face. Dick Tidrow and Cecil Upshaw were already in there."

And then it happened.

"He told us we were traded. This is a Friday night. I was shocked. I come out of his office and the celebration has cooled. It was a large trade because it was a seven-player deal and they were getting four pitchers back. At that time, Cleveland didn't have a lot of pitching, but we had a lot of good hitting."

Chris Chambliss

The very next morning, Chambliss was on a plane bound for New York.

"I think it was a one o'clock game and I was in a Yankee uniform at Shea Stadium. It was just a severe shock."

Gone!

Here is Chris Chambliss' description of one of the biggest home runs in Yankee history.

"I knew I hit it deep. It was one of those ones that was hit high and it was hit not too far from the wall, really. It didn't go over by very much.

"McRae went to the wall looking like it might come down in his glove but it went just over that fence. It wasn't one of those that you hit and you know that it is gone. The one like that that I really enjoyed was my World Series home run. When I hit that, I knew it was gone. This one, I didn't know it was gone."

9/11

Chris Chambliss, having completed his season as the Marlins' Triple-A manager in Calgary, was invited to Florida to join the major league coaching staff for the final month of the 2001 season.

He had an early morning flight from Newark to Fort Lauderdale on Tuesday, September 11. That means he may possibly have been in the take-off line in front of United Flight 93, one of the doomed planes that was to be commandeered by hijackers that crashed near Shanksville, Pennsylvania at 10:10 a.m.

"The flight was somewhere around 8:15. While we're up in the air, a lady right behind me is looking out the window on the left-hand side that faces the Manhattan skyline. I turned around and she said that the World Trade Center was smoking."

At that point, Chambliss and his fellow passengers had no idea about the mayhem that was going on.

"A little later on in the flight, the pilot told us that we were going to land in Durham. He assured us it was nothing mechanical and said he would explain more when we landed."

Chambliss was instructed to get his luggage out of baggage claim and leave the airport premises as soon as possible. A phone call home told him all he needed to know about the worst terrorist attack ever on American soil.

"I got a hotel room, stayed there three days, and was in touch with the team. They were to play home games on the 11th, 12th and 13th and then play in Atlanta over the weekend. If they were gonna play those games, I was gonna rent a car and drive there from Durham."

Of course, those games were postponed too.

"Once we found that out, I rented a car anyway and drove north back home to New Jersey. Just so happened my parents live in Alexandria, Virginia, so I drove about five hours to their house and stayed with them for the weekend. Then I drove home."

By this time, the season was resuming.

"The Marlins started up in Montreal. It would have been impossible to get there through international flying. After there, they were to go to Philadelphia which was only a train ride away for me. That's what I did later that week to meet the club and ended up spending the rest of the season with them."

Chris Chambliss puts it all in perspective this way:

"The ordeal was nothing was compared to what everybody else went through. I was just very fortunate."

Safe at Home... Wherever it May Be

In the wake of the pandemonium that greeted Chris Chambliss' pennant-winning home run, everything on the Stadium that could be taken was. That included home plate.

"The first thing that happened was when I came around second base. I tripped right after I hit the bag. I don't know why, I just tripped. I quickly got back up."

It's not every day one worries about getting trampled after one hits a home run.

"People were all over the place. I remember, and I've seen a picture of it, someone trying to grab my helmet. I don't know what made me do it but I grabbed my helmet and tucked it away like a football. Third base was just a mob of people so I kind of went around them toward the outfield and just swung around in front of the Royals dugout. I was in a full sprint then straight into our dugout. I was just dodging people. I just remember somebody in front of me that I must have forearmed or something and just stepped over him and headed to the dugout."

And the clubhouse where everybody asked him if he ever touched home plate.

"I said no way did I touch it because there were a bunch of people around. Nobody hardly knows this, but I put on a jacket and took two security cops in uniform and the three of us went through the crowd. While people were still jumping around near home plate, I put my foot on the area where it was. No umpire saw it but we did it anyway and went back in the clubhouse. It was really wild."

JACK CLARK

'Jack the Ripper' Nervous?

In 1987, playing for the National League champion St. Louis Cardinals, Jack Clark, the main cog in their offensive machine, struck 35 homers, had 106 RBIs and led the league in slugging percentage and walks before an ankle injury ended his season September 9. A contract squabble was all he needed to take his free-agent walk to the Bronx, even though someone with the initials Don Mattingly was ensconced at first.

"To be honest with you, I was a little nervous. For one thing, it was the American League and it was the New York Yankees. You're talking about one of the elite franchises, along with the Celtics and a few other teams, in sports."

He had to re-learn everything, from the umpires to the pitchers to the cities and the ballparks. And there was something else.

"George Steinbrenner could be a little scary because you didn't know what to expect."

Even though he hit .242, his lowest average in a full season, Clark had led the team with 27 homers and escaped The Boss' wrath.

"I'll tell you what, George was great to me. He treated me well and was so gracious. He went out his way to make me feel comfortable and to become a Yankee."

But Clark's heart was left in San Francisco . . . and St. Louis.

"I was one of those guys who should not have switched leagues. But that was because of collusion and a lot of other things that were going on at the time. I was real fortunate to have an opportunity under the circumstances when collusion was going on to get a job anywhere, let alone with the Yankees.

"When George signed me, that kind of opened up the market. George, God bless him, broke through the barrier because he's a man and he wants to win and he wants to win for the City of New York and he wants the best players and he wants to do what this country is based on, having the right to do and say what you want to do. He didn't like not being able to do that. So by bringing me over there, he got in a little bit of trouble but he also stood up for something that was right."

Jack Clark thinks George Steinbrenner doesn't get the credit he deserves.

"People don't understand that, yeah, he's fired a lot of people. But people should tip their hat on what he has been able to do. All he has ever wanted to do is win and bring World Championships to the greatest city and the greatest organization in baseball and that's New York."

Hanging By a Thread

There is one story from his time with the Yankees that Jack Clark will always remember.

"I've tried to explain to people the character of Billy Martin, what a tough bastard he was. If he was on your side, you couldn't have a better guy.

"We were in Texas and it was about two o'clock in the morning and the kitchen in the hotel caught on fire. I remember the alarms going off and they wanted everybody out of the hotel.

"The hotel was situated right by Six Flags and the water park, so there was a lot of children and families there on vacation.

"They brought everybody downstairs to the lobby so players were down there with shorts on, some with slacks and a T-shirt. People had been sleeping or watching TV. The kids were there in their pajamas and slippers. The players were kind of getting hounded by the kids for autographs."

That's when George Steinbrenner, who happened to be on site, took matters into his own hands.

"He had the players separated for security and had everybody herded into the bar to have privacy."

And then the cab showed up.

"It's two o'clock in the morning and this cab pulls up and it's Billy getting out of the cab. His shirt's all bloody and his ear is just about hanging off of his head. It looked like he had just gotten out of a boxing match. He was all puffy around his face which was contorted. It was so twisted, like there was a big split in his head.

"Billy had a white shirt and tie on, all of which was completely bloody.

"He came in and the kids were screaming. George rushed him into the bar and the trainers told him they needed to get him to a hospital."

That's not what Billy needed.

"He sat down and wanted a drink. He didn't want to go to the hospital until they got him a drink. George put his foot down and said, 'Get him the hell out of here.' That meant guys picking him up if they had to in order to put him in a cab or ambulance or whatever."

Billy eventually left. But there was a ballgame to be played the next night.

"Billy showed up a little bit late, but he came. He got in the Jacuzzi, he was all bandaged up, he looked like a mummy. To his credit, he put his uniform on, went out there and took the line-up card with his ear taped back up to the side of his head and his eyes black and blue. He could barely see. I don't know whether we won or lost, but I know we tried the best we could under those circumstances."

Raised Expectations

Before coming to New York, Jack Clark played in two organizations with great histories, the Giants and the Cardinals.

Being with the Yankees, however, was different.

"I never have felt that I wanted to win or try to win or needed to win like here. I mean, the games in spring training were important. That's what I remember, the tradition of the Yankees and how important winning was."

Clark liked what he saw.

"People can talk about it and they can say we want to win. They can say we expect to win. But can they show it on a daily basis with the pride and the tradition to actually walk their talk?

"The Yankees do and George Steinbrenner does, the city does and they have a lot to be proud of. I'm just really fortunate to be able to say that in my career I had an opportunity to wear the pinstripes and be a New York Yankees. I'm very proud of that. I wouldn't want it any other way. They epitomized sport, let alone baseball. It doesn't get any better than that."

There's something about that uni.

"You feel and sense a pride, how you're supposed to carry yourself. It takes over. You have to be pretty tough, pretty strong because there's a lot that's expected. But once you find out how to do it and how to carry yourself and try to fit in there, there's not a better place in sports to be."

In a five-team race, Jack Clark's 1988 Yankees faded at the end of the season, finishing fifth in the East, but only 3 1/2 games behind Boston. He was traded back to the National League to San Diego that winter for pitchers Lance McCullers and Jimmy Jones and outfielder Stanley Jefferson.

BOBBY COX

The unheralded Bobby Cox, who has won with all different types of teams in Atlanta, will forever hold the Yankees close to his heart. For it all started for him in pinstripes.

Cox left eight long years in the minors behind him when he was acquired by the Yankees, along with fellow third baseman, Mike Ferraro, in the winter of 1967.

The following spring, Manager Ralph Houk had them do battle. Cox scuffled, while Ferraro was on fire and won the job.

As the team flew home to New York, someone showed Mickey Mantle the stat sheet. Ferraro had batted about .353, about four points higher than Mantle.

Mickey yelled out, "Hey, Mike, you led the club in hitting." Ferraro yelled back, "Who'd you expect?"

But it was Cox who started on Opening Day. It might as well have been yesterday.

"It was against the Detroit Tigers. I can remember the pitcher was Joe Sparma and I can remember the national anthem in the old Yankee Stadium before they refurbished it. I was at attention saluting the flag during the anthem. I went up on my tippy-toes to stretch a little bit and I got some cramps in the back of my legs. I got a basehit off Sparma, I hit a line-drive off him. The old tradition in Yankee Stadium, packed house on Opening Day. Babe Ruth, Gehrig and Mantle and all those people."

'68 was to be Mantle's final season, parked at first base, taking throws from Bobby Cox.

"You know, I'm in the Hall of Fame as well as Mickey because I was involved in a triple play with him. The bases were loaded and Dooley Womack was pitching. Someone hit a line-drive to him, he threw to me at third and I threw back to Mickey and we got a triple play. The ball got to the Hall of Fame. So I can say I'm in Cooperstown with the Mick."

RON DAVIS

A Real Pay Toilet

Goose Gossage heeded the call innings before he was expected to heed the call.

"It's 1980 and it was getting late in the ballgame. We were playing the Angels. It was about the sixth inning and Gossage went into the restroom. You have to put the door from the inside to get out."

Wouldn't you know it, there just happened to be a metal cable handy.

"I wrapped it around the door and tied it to the stairwell. Well, the phone rings and they say, 'Gossage, get up, get ready to throw.' Well, he jerked the door and that cable singed very tight. We couldn't get him out of the rest room. So they call back and say, 'RD, you get up.'"

While workmen were scouring the Stadium for a handy pair of wire-cutters to extricate the Goose, 'RD' was in the game on fire.

"I struck out all three in the eighth, got two outs in the ninth and Howser walks out in the ninth and pulls me. Goose comes in and gets the save."

Dick Howser fined Ron Davis $500 for his hijinks.

No Wonder They Run in From the Bullpen

"We were in Milwaukee. They'd drive you in from the bullpen in a Firebird around the pads and stop and you'd get out and run to the mound. They called down to get Gossage up to start the ninth inning."

The Yanks are out and it's time for a Goose with a twist.

"He walks down to the car. You usually get in on the passenger side. He opens the door on the driver's side and takes the driver out of the car. He get in the car, closes the door, turns up the radio, revs up the engine, the wheels are spinning and there's rocks shooting out from underneath and there's smoke. Right before he hits the grass, he does a left turn and just floors it all the way around right field until he gets in front of the first-base dugout which was Milwaukee's."

By this time, Davis estimates Gossage is probably going 45 to 50.

"He hits the brakes and starts a skid of about 30 feet on the side on the rocks. Dust and gravel is flying into their dugout. He comes out and there's smoke everywhere and the engine's throbbing. He jumps out of the car, runs out to the mound, throws nine pitches, strikes three guys out, game over."

BUCKY DENT

Just Call Me Babe

So what was the biggest swing that Bucky Dent ever had in his life prior to October 2, 1978 in the seventh inning in Boston, Massachusetts?

"To tell you the truth, I hit a home run in the All-Star Game for Cal Ripken Sr. in Double-A. I think it was the All-Stars against Montgomery. I think I hit the home run in the top of the ninth inning.

"It was as surprising then as the one in Boston."

Something to Remember Me By

Imagine what the life of Russell Earl Dent would be like if he never hammered that up-and-in fastball from Mike Torrez into the net above the Green Monster one late fall afternoon.

"The only thing it did was make me more visible. It was a big game that people remember and they remember me for it. As far as my life changing, I don't think anything would have changed except that people remember who I am and where they were when it happened."

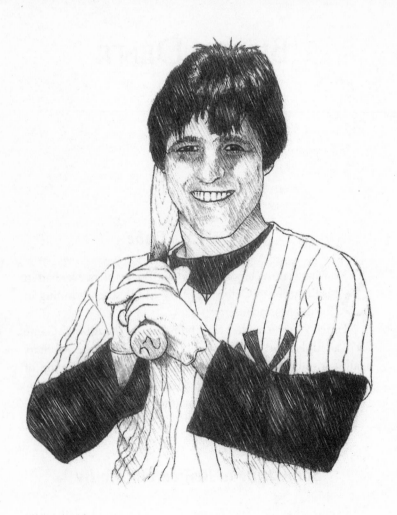

Bucky Dent

Has it ever been a burden?

"No, never. It's been a lot of fun because you meet a lot of different people who talk about it all the time and how it changed their lives. People talk about driving off the road. It's fun talking to those people because they can remember where they were and what they were doing at that time."

And it's a real goof every time he's in New England.

"Oh yeah, it is."

You have a new middle initial.

"Oh yeah," he said laughing. "F."

AL DEVORMER

Backup catcher Al DeVormer spent an undistinguished 46-game career with the Yankees in 1921 and 1922. Most notable about the Michigan native—besides his occasional agitation in the clubhouse—was his penchant for doing crazy things.

On one occasion, DeVormer jumped into Lake Michigan in his street clothes just to win a $25 bet.

BILL DICKEY

Best Catcher?

B ill Dickey is often referred to as the best Yankee catcher
of all time, impressive considering his heady company.
He hit better than .300 for 11 seasons.

Wrote Dan Daniel: "Dickey isn't just a catcher. He's a ball
club. He isn't just a player. He's an influence."

In Control

Dickey was a tough ballplayer behind the dish. On July 4,
1932, a collision took place between Dickey and Carl Reynolds
of Washington. Words were exchanged and Dickey broke
Reynolds' jaw with a single punch.

Dickey was fined $1,000 and sat out a month.

JOE DIMAGGIO

The Streak

Baseball historians have argued over what baseball record will go down next. Mark McGwire and Sammy Sosa played their part in eclipsing Roger Maris' 61-homer record during a glorious 1998 season.

Near the end of the 1998 season, Baltimore Orioles infielder Cal Ripken Jr. put a coda on the consecutive games streak that he had lifted from the Iron Horse, Yankee great Lou Gehrig.

That leaves Joe DiMaggio's 56-game consecutive hitting streak in 1941 near the top of everyone's list.

"The streak," as it became known, started quietly on May 15 and culminated with a record crowd on July 17. DiMaggio's feats lifted a nation, which was poised on the brink of world war. His batting average stood at .306 when DiMaggio stepped up to face Chicago White Sox left-hander Edgar Smith.

DiMaggio singled in the first inning, a simple act which opened a drama that would catch the attention of a nation. In fact, the streak wasn't noticed for weeks.

A month into the streak, DiMaggio's legendary status grew, as did his popularity. He was swarmed by well-wishers as he attended the Joe Louis-Billy Conn heavyweight title fight.

"There were so many people asking for his autograph that he had almost as many cops around him as the fighters," friend George Solotaire said.

Joe DiMaggio

While some pitchers took to pitching away from DiMaggio—not a bad idea considering his average was in the .350 range—others did not fear him, and usually paid for it.

St. Louis Browns rookie Bob Muncrief served up an eighth-inning single to stretch the streak to 36. Browns manager Luke Sewell demanded to know why he decided to pitch to DiMaggio. Said Muncrief: "I wasn't going to walk him. That wouldn't have been fair—to him or to me. Hell, he's the greatest player I ever saw."

Even when pitchers threw away from DiMaggio, sometimes luck and a little skill were on his side. Johnny Babich of the Philadelphia A's was ready to serve up a walk when DiMaggio reached for an outside pitch and lined a shot through Babich's legs. Noted DiMaggio: "(Manager Joe) McCarthy was great to me during the streak. He let me hit the 3-0 pitch quite a few times."

Even DiMaggio's teammates came to his aid. With the streak on the line against the Browns, McCarthy granted Tommy Henrich's request for an eighth-inning bunt to avoid a potential double-play ball that likely would have put an end to DiMaggio's streak. Henrich sacrificed and DiMaggio then doubled on the first delivery from Eldon Auker.

In Washington, D.C., a fan stole DiMaggio's bat, the one he had just used to tie George Sisler's American League record streak of 41. DiMaggio was upset because he had taken some precious weight off the 36-inch, 36-ounce piece of wood with sandpaper. Fortunately, friends of DiMaggio later recovered the bat from the Newark, New Jersey, fan who had lifted it and then made the mistake of bragging about it.

The streak came to an end on July 17 at Cleveland Stadium. A taxi driver had taken DiMaggio and pitcher Lefty Gomez to the ballpark. His words to DiMaggio proved prophetic. "I got a feeling that if you don't get a hit the first time up, they're gonna stop you tonight," the driver said, raising Gomez's dander a bit. "What the hell is this?" he demanded. "What are you trying to do—jinx him?"

Indians third baseman Ken Keltner robbed DiMaggio of hits in the first and seventh innings. In the eighth, reliever Jim Bagby Jr. came on to face DiMaggio. He hit a shot that short-stop Lou Boudreau fielded off a bad hop to start a double play.

New York Sun writer Herb Goren wrote the next day: "DiMaggio rounded first base, picked up his glove and trotted to center field. There was no kicking of dirt, no shaking of the head."

The Other Streak

The 56-game streak was not DiMaggio's longest. He hit in 61 consecutive games with the San Francisco Seals of the Pacific Coast League in 1933.

Threaded

Image was always important for Joe DiMaggio, and he dressed the part wearing fine suits. In 1936, he was voted one of the 10 best-dressed men in America.

And Now, The Lyrics

In the midst of the 56-game hitting streak, a disc jockey named Alan Courtney penned lyrics to honor Joe DiMaggio. His copyrighted tune "Jolting Joe DiMaggio" goes like this:

> *Who started baseball's famous streak*
> *That's got us all aglow?*

He's just a man and not a freak.
Jolting Joe DiMaggio.
Joe. . . Joe. . . DiMaggio. . .
we want you on our side.
From Coast to Coast, that's all you hear
Of Joe the One-Man Show.
He's glorified the horsehide sphere,
Jolting Joe DiMaggio.
Joe. . . Joe. . . DiMaggio . . .
we want you on our side.
He'll live in baseball's Hall of Fame.
He got there blow-by-blow
Our kids will tell their kids his name.
Jolting Joe DiMaggio.

Big City? Hah!

Joe DiMaggio retired at the age of 36.

In an address to fans on Joe DiMaggio Day in 1949, he spoke of being made welcome. "When I was in San Francisco, Lefty O'Doul told me: 'Joe, don't let the big city scare you. New York is the friendliest town in the world.' This day proves it. I want to thank my fans, my friends, my manager, Casey Stengel; my teammates, the gamest, fightingest bunch of guys that ever lived. And I want to thank the good Lord for making me a Yankee."

On The Big Screen

Joe DiMaggio made his Hollywood debut in 1937 in a movie called "Manhattan Merry-Go Round." He also appeared in the 1951 film "Angels in the Outfield."

AL DOWNING

The Only Game in Town

When Al Downing signed a professional contract with the Yankees in 1961, they were the only game in town.

"You have understand the times that were happening in baseball. The Dodgers had both gone to the West Coast in '58. Not only were the only team in New York, they were basically the kings of the major leagues. That's not to be facetious. They were a ballclub that epitomized baseball. And when you stop and think about it, a lot of the legislation that came about subsequently was aimed at the success of the Yankees such as the free-agent draft, expansion and stuff like that. You had the freedom to sign with whomever you wanted to when I did. You signed with the best ballclub. The best ballclub was the Yankees."

But there was more to it than that.

"The Giants had sent somebody to look at me, the Washington Senators did the same thing, the Pittsburgh Pirates and the Phillies. But there was a common attraction. The fellow who tried to sign me for the Phillies when I came out of high school signed me a year-and-a-half later for the Yankees. That's pretty much how I wound up with the Yankees. It wasn't as if they were knocking my door down. It was because of this one particular scout that I signed with the Yankees."

Guesswork

Al Downing held opponents to a league-low .184 average his first year in the majors in 1963 and led the league in strikeouts with 217 in his second. Hard to believe he didn't know what he was doing on the mound. Could've fooled us.

"In my own mind I was disappointed that I didn't have better success. As I look back in retrospect, someone once said that youth is wasted on the young. I felt that I didn't learn how to pitch until I had been in the major leagues about five years. I always use that as a yardstick because you basically don't know what you're doing. So you're pretty much pitching on anxiety and instinct, not knowledge because you don't have much knowledge. That's why I don't feel that I had great success because I felt that my better years were still ahead of me."

Then Al Downing hurt his arm in 1967.

BRIAN DOYLE

What's a Brian Doyle?

That was the reaction in the Yankee clubhouse when it was learned that Willie Randolph would miss the 1978 postseason with a hamstring injury.

"That's exactly right. I had been up and down seven times that year.

"I was called up the last time when the rosters expanded so I was ineligible for postseason play. The Yankees had to get a special permission from the Commissioner's Office and from the Kansas City Royals, who we were facing in the playoffs, for me to be eligible for the postseason roster. They gave that permission because of the question everyone was asking: what's a Brian Doyle? I had to go through the same procedure for the World Series and they asked the same question."

Brian Doyle provided the answer: a .423 average, with six hits in the final two games. The 262-point differential between his Series average and lifetime average of .161 is the greatest among players with his number of at-bats in the history of baseball.

Notice? I Don't Need No Stinkin' Notice!

"I did not know that I was going to be playing in the World Series until the day of the first game. I got in the cab to go to Dodger Stadium with Yogi. He said, 'Looks like you're gonna be playing, kid.' That was the first I had heard of it. So I didn't know until just hours before the game."

It's not as if Doyle had time to be nervous...because he doesn't get nervous.

"I have never been nervous on a baseball field. What I was more concerned with was keeping my adrenaline down because of the excitement. With the whole family in professional baseball, this could be a once in a lifetime experience. I was excited and just couldn't wait for the chance."

Up and Down and Up and Down and Up and Down and Up and Down and Up and Down and Up and Down and Up and Down

In 1978, Brian Doyle was recalled by the Yankees an astonishing seven different times from Triple-A. The farm club was conveniently located that one season in Tacoma, Washington.

"It was amazing just going back and forth and trying to raise a family having a little son. That was the real pressure. The pressure wasn't the World Series. The pressure was being away from my family and trying to pay bills. And everybody in America understands that type of pressure. So when we got to the World Series, everybody kept on asking, 'Why aren't you nervous?' I'd say, 'I'm not nervous at all' and they'd go, 'Oh yeah, right.' Here's this young kid in a World Series and not nervous. But seriously, I wasn't because of the separation from my family, trying to pay two types of housing bills and meet the monthly bills. That's real pressure when you're flying cross country seven different times and the wife and the son is in limbo. Finally, at the end, I just flew them back to Kentucky with his mother and said, 'Don't move till you hear from me.'"

The overall experience was disconcerting.

"Professionally speaking, it was so difficult, especially for a little guy like myself who was always known as not a lot of pop with the bat but a good contact hitter. To be a good contact hitter and to produce, you have to have continual at-bats."

Which wasn't happening.

"I'd go and sit on the Yankee bench for three weeks at a time and then I'd go back to Triple-A and get some at-bats and then two weeks later I was back doing the same thing in New York again. It was disheartening. Sure, it was great to be in the big leagues and all of them but it was a very difficult situation."

The Yankees saw Doyle as insurance and not a whole lot more than that.

"That's exactly right. They knew that I could catch the ball, throw the ball and turn the double-play and I knew that I could do that with anybody in the game."

A Hairy Comeback

In 1995, Brian Doyle was diagnosed with a rare form of cancer, Hairy Cell Leukemia. Of course, the experience changed his life.

"I have always considered myself strong in my faith. But when something like that happens, reality really, really hits and you find out how strong your faith is. It was just life-changing experience knowing that because of the faith that's in me and the God that I believe in and lives in me that I could go through that."

Doyle had to go through very drastic treatment.

"I was the guinea pig. I was the first person to do double treatments and I did that for almost two years. There was a lot of prayer. One unknown author said, 'Baseball is life with the volume turned up.'

"When the doctor said I was in the final stages of leukemia, it was because of my life in baseball and all of those ups and downs and disheartening consequences."

Here's his message:

"I'm here. When I woke up this morning, I got one day to do something positive for somebody else. That's how it affected me. I got one more day. I don't look at tomorrow like I used to because the moment I live is right now. I remember a good friend of mine saying, 'Use the good china.'"

You're welcome, Brian. Three years later, I was diagnosed with cancer.

With no symptoms and no history of cancer in the family.

January 20, 2002 was the seventh anniversary of Brian Doyle being cancer free.

DOUG DRABEK

What a start! Doug Drabek, a pitcher Yankee fans still lament from a time the ballclub would habitually eat their young, had quite a debut in pinstripes in 1986. After starting 1-4 with a 7.29 ERA in eight games for AAA Columbus, hardly numbers worthy of a call-up, Drabek was nonetheless summoned to the big club.

His first start came against Baltimore for Manager Lou Piniella, but as Drabek arrived at the ballpark, he had no idea he would get the ball.

"There were two balls in my locker. I said, 'Geez, you make it up here and they give you a brand-new ball.'"

Drabek pitched into the fifth inning when he was removed *without having allowed a hit and only one baserunner, a walk.*

"The first guy in the fifth got on on an error and I walked the next guy," said Drabek. "I didn't think anything of being taken out because I thought they gave the guy a hit. After the game, somebody brought it to my attention. That's the first I knew I hadn't given up a hit. But I was just happy to have a chance to start."

Drabek was 7-8 his rookie season for a second-place Yankee team that finished 90-72, 5 1/2 games behind Boston. He was then traded that November with reliever Brian Fisher and a minor leaguer (where have you gone, Logan Easley?) for pitchers Rick Rhoden, Cecilio Guante and Pat Clements. Four years later, Drabek won 22 games for Pittsburgh and was named the National League Cy Young Award winner.

RYNE DUREN

That'll Show 'Em

R yne Duren can't remember the exact first time it
happened but he does recall 1958 as being the year in
which he began firing his first warm-up pitch onto the
screen behind home plate.

"That's the season Bob Turley had the great year. For some
reason or another, he didn't like much drop in the mound. He
liked it a little flat, maybe because he kind of came from the
side. He went to the groundcrew and asked them if they could
make less slope in front of the rubber."

Duren was warming up in the bullpen where that mound
had a very different feel.

"You released the ball in coordination with when your foot
came down. What I did was kind of like the artillery: you fired
the first one and then zeroed in from there. I came in and threw
that first ball real hard. I thought my knee was gonna hit my
chest. But my foot got down so fast I had to release the ball or I'd
tear myself apart. The foot triggers the release. So that ball went
way up on the screen. That's how it happened the first time."

Casey Stengel, Frank Crosetti and the press corps thought it
was great.

Did he do it in every game?

"Absolutely not. I would do it every once in a while for the
hell of it. This was after I was well established. I sure wouldn't

want to do it as a rookie. Nobody likes a smart-ass rookie, you know how that goes.

"Crosetti always thought it was great. He always thought it intimidated the opposition. I never felt so."

A Most Unlikely Scenario

During the 1961 season, the Yankees traded Ryne Duren to the expansion Los Angeles Angels for pitcher Tex Clevinger and to reacquire outfielder Bob Cerv. Later on that season, Duren was taken out of the bullpen to start against Turley.

"Bill Rigney thought, 'Maybe Duren's got something to prove.' In the sixth inning, they were beating me one to nothing. Mantle had a grounder and I had to cover first. He carried me across first base and down the right field line so as not to run over me. Kubek scored from second base."

In the bottom of the sixth inning, the Angels had the bases loaded and Duren was the due hitter.

"If there was one out, Rigney would have had to pinch-hit for me. But since I was pitching well, he let me hit. Turley got two quick strikes on me and he kind of nodded as if trying to get me thinking."

Duren says you never pitch a guy with glasses up in his eyes. Turley did.

"He threw another fastball, this one out of the strike zone and a little bit high. I hit that choked-up-bat grounder right past him and Kubek and Richardson both just about got it before it rolled into centerfield for a single. Two to one. Then little Albie Pearson came up behind me and hit the first pitch out of the ballpark into the short right field bleachers in the old LA park. People in the stands went crazy from the time I hit that ball until the ballgame was over. I think I was relieved in the eighth inning and got the win."

When Bill Rigney died last year, his daughter called Duren and told him that of all of the things that happened while he was in baseball, he talked about that the most.

MIKE EASLER

Why Don't Men Ask for Directions?

M ike Easler had just had a wonderful day for the
Boston Red Sox. In a spring training exhibition
game against the Mets, he had gone 2-for-3 with
a home run off Dwight Gooden. This was the 1986 Gooden,
purveyor of high octane gas.

"I had just gotten home. It was about 5:30, 6 o'clock. I got
a call from Lou Gorman, the General Manager, saying I was
traded to the Yankees. Wow! I had stuff spread everywhere in
my apartment. I ended up taking off from Winter Haven for
Fort Lauderdale. I left about seven or eight that night and ended
up in Key West. I drove all night long and got there about seven
or eight in the morning."

At ten o'clock, Mike Easier reported for spring training.

"Lou Piniella says, 'How do you feel?' I said, 'I feel great.' He
says, 'Can you play right field today?' I'm a DH. I say, 'Sure,
whatever.' I hit the ball pretty doggone good."

Sure A World Championship is Nice, But. . .

The player known as the 'Hit Man' was a valued member
of the 1979 World Champion 'We Are Familee' Pittsburgh

Pirates. But that was before he came to New York to play well for the Yankees.

"It was the greatest experience an athlete can have. I think every ballplayer that plays the game and makes it to the major leagues should play in New York at least one or two years. That's when you reach the top of your profession when you play with one of the New York teams."

The fact that the fans are so demanding fired him up.

"There's the pressure day in and day out, the demands of the fans. The organization is bent on winning, and winning is what it's all about. And when you go there, you can't ever go through the motions. You always have to play at your height. To me, that was the greatest experience of my career in the major leagues.

Even more than Pittsburgh?

"Oh God, yes, it was totally different in New York. You got the media, you got the fans and their love for the game. It's a different love for the game that they have in New York. It's a passion and it's what a true ballplayer should have anyway. You should play with pride and integrity and give everything that you have."

DOCK ELLIS

A Throw-In

When the Yankees set their sights on the Pittsburgh Pirates as a trading partner in the winter of 1975, the object of their affection was a Triple-A second baseman from Brooklyn by the name of Willie Randolph.

"They wouldn't trade Willie unless the Yankees took me. The Pirates had to get me out of there. I had worn out my welcome. Danny Murtaugh and I didn't see eye to eye on certain things. The General Manager for the Pirates, Joe Brown, made a bet with the Yankees General Manager, that I would win more than 12 games."

Joe Brown was right. Dock Ellis won 17 games and one more in the playoffs.

Rabbit Ears

"One game that stands out from that 1976 season was a start I had in Milwaukee. I pitched against Bill Travers and lost like 1-0 or 2-0. But the thing I remember about it was these three little old ladies who sat behind home plate and they were calling my pitchers."

Ellis said they were there for every game, rain or shine. He estimated they were at least in their 60s.

"They would give little signs. Sometimes they would scream out, 'Throw that fastball, Dock, throw that fastball.' Or 'Throw that sinker, throw that sinker. He can't hit the sinker, throw it to him.' Or they would say, 'It's time for the pitch, it's time for the pitch.' In that particular game, I don't know if the wind was blowing right or whatever but I could hear their every whim. I used to be rabbit eyes when I was younger but after that, I couldn't hear anything. But those ladies I could hear."

The Circus is in Town

For Dock Ellis, there was nothing like playing for the New York Yankees.

"It really didn't dawn on me until years later what guys dreamed to do. And that was to play for the Yankees. I don't what it is. It was totally different. I had been with the Pirates and we would come in and kick butt every day with The Lumber Company and stuff. But with the Yankees, you were on exhibit. It was like people just came to look at you. They were in awe of you."

As Dock says, "You had to do what you had to do.

"You had to sign all the autographs, you had to talk baseball to the people and if you're in New York, you had to make sure to ask them if they were a Yankee fan or a Met fan. Or are you just over here to watch us and you're a Met fan?"

JOHNNY ELLIS

Johnny Ellis, a strong-as-bull catcher in the late 60s, was afflicted with Hodgkin's Disease. Now cancer-free, he has taken darkness and transformed it into light.

"The issues that surrounded my decision to turn my problem around was quite simply this. My brother and sister had died of cancer, one from Hodgkins, the other from lymphoma both before the age of 40. Subsequently, before I was 40, I was diagnosed with Hodgkins, stage four. At stage five, there is not too much hope."

Ellis' doctor performed what he called "medical protocol", a fancy term for experimentation.

"While sitting in this dark room thinking about what I have missed in life, I really couldn't think of anything else and that's the truth. Not expecting to live, I really didn't use any mind therapy that patients use to fight cancer."

That's when Johnny Ellis made a commitment.

"I made a deal with whoever you make a deal with while you have tubes in you and a bunch of other stuff because I had had a few operations during this period of time. I said, 'Lookit, if I get a chance to live I'm going to help needy cancer families and also fund cancer research.' So not expecting to live, I thought it was a fair deal."

Ellis had seen the devastating financial effects of the disease close-up.

"During that period of time when my brother went through his bout with cancer, he was a teacher in our school system in Connecticut. His insurance limits reached their ceilings and subsequently, he did not have enough money to fight cancer. So as a family, we had to put money in to help his fight, things like paying for his home and taking care of his medicines. So I really felt that there was a need."

As Johnny Ellis began to survive and get his treatments for cancer, he saw other people far worse off than he was. They did not have the financial wherewithal to fight the disease.

"People afflicted with cancer who are the breadwinners in the family, if they don't have enough money to pay their bills, the psychological build-up, the piling-on of your problems become greater sometimes than your will to live. And this is, in itself, a problem in fighting cancer.

"If you wanted me to weigh the percentage of lifesaving force versus the financial benefit or treatment, I'd have to say that having the financial strength is equal to getting the best treatment possible."

Ellis says a lot of people were compromised under this pressure.

"I was going through this treatment and seeing all these people collapsing under this pressure, people who were not coming back the next day. So as I began to survive my own therapy to treat my cancer, I went out and formed a foundation."

This is long before that became commonplace for contemporary athletes.

"I asked Mickey Mantle, Whitey Ford and Billy Martin to come to my first dinner. We raised $150,000."

That was in the late 80s. Since then, Johnny Ellis has raised in the vicinity of four or five million dollars.

"I made a pact with whoever you make you pact with. I said I better live up to it."

Literally.

WHITEY FORD

Oh, Waiter . . .

When Whitey Ford and Mickey Mantle got together, their teammates had to prep for any practical joke. When Joe Pepitone and Phil Linz made the club, Ford and Mantle told the new guys to get dressed up and meet them at a Detroit restaurant called The Flame.

Ford and Mantle were going to pick up the tab. All they had to do was ask for Mantle's favorite table.

Pepitone and Linz were so excited about being invited to dinner with the team leaders they told everyone about it.

A half-hour cab ride was the capper to the cruelest joke.

The establishment was in the middle of an urban slum. A sign over the door read: THE FLAME. No Mantle. No Ford. No table.

The Craftsmen

Whitey Ford won 236 games in 16 seasons with the Yankees, with 10 more coming in World Series play. The crafty left-hander used every trick in his arsenal to baffle hitters.

The mud ball, or "mudder" as it was known, was positively vicious as it sailed in or out, up or down on hitters.

Whitey Ford

Catcher Ellie Howard was Ford's accomplice, often loading the ball up with mud before throwing it back to the mound. He'd cover it up by pretending to lose his balance and righting himself with his hand while the ball was in it.

Ford also liked to use his wedding ring. By gouging slices into the ball, a pitch could dive down, sail up or take a little hop before reaching the plate. When that trick was discovered, Howard would use the buckle on his shin guards to nick the ball.

How Do You Spell Relief?

When Ford was pitching on the hill, there was little need to go to the relief staff. To keep his bullpen pals happy, Ford would set up a table in the bullpen, cover it with a checkered tablecloth and place a candle on it. He would then treat his fellow hurlers to some hero sandwiches.

Hit? Where?

Whitey Ford used his sharp wit on his teammates. In 1965, Leon James "Duke" Carmel was a phenom waiting to bust loose, except his bat wouldn't support the claims of Yankee scouts.

Carmel struggled during spring training games in Fort Lauderdale, Florida, prompting Ford to say, "Well, Duke, it looks like you can't hit in southern Florida."

A trip to Tampa didn't help. "Well, Duke, it looks like you're just not a Florida hitter," Ford said.

A few more exhibition games in the South didn't yield hits, either. "Well, Duke, it looks like you just can't hit south of the Mason-Dixon Line."

A 0-for-8 effort in six regular-season games was all the Yankees needed to see to release Carmel.

Golden Arm

October. World Series. Yankee great Whitey Ford on the hill.

It was commonplace.

"You kind of took it for granted around the Yankees that there was always going to be baseball in October," Ford said.

His Yankee teams won 11 American League pennants, allowing Ford the opportunity to start a record 22 World Series games.

Money Ahead

In his retirement speech, Ford said, "I came here in 1950 and I was wearing $50 suits. And I'm leaving wearing $200 suits. And I'm getting' 'em for $80. So I guess I'm doing all right."

One Wasn't Enough

Most players earn one nickname during their career. Edward Charles Ford had three: Whitey, Slick and Chairman of the Board.

The Winningest

Ford racked up the most wins in Yankee history, so he always had a warm spot for pitchers of the Senior Circuit. After pitching the clincher of the 1950 World Series against the Phillies, Ford ran into broadcaster Dizzy Dean, formerly of the St. Louis Cardinals. "No wonder you won 30 games," Ford told him. "You were pitching in that crummy National League. I would win 40 in that league myself."

OSCAR GAMBLE

About That House...

A fter being reacquired by the Yankees, Oscar Gamble spent much of the 1983 season living in a hotel. All the while he had his sights set on a house owned by disgruntled teammate Jerry Mumphrey. Often he'd playfully feed Mumphrey's frustrations in hopes Mumphrey would demand a trade.

"How much longer are you going to live in that hotel?" someone asked Gamble.

"Right up until the time Mumphrey gets traded."

Humor At The End Of The Bench

Gamble never was satisfied with the playing time he received, but he always maintained his quick wit.

Told he was batting fifth in one game, Gamble said, "I guess that's better than hitting 12th, where I have been playing."

While razzing Lou Piniella, Gamble said, "When you come up, the left fielder takes a cigarette break. You can't pull the ball anymore. They're going to pull the old Satchel Paige routine on you. Pull all the outfielders in and sit them around the mound."

Quick! Draw!

For a while, Gamble was known as "Jesse" to some players.

During contract negotiations with the San Diego Padres one season, Gamble was ready to ask for $1.5 million. Owner Ray Kroc stepped in and gave Gamble a contract ultimatum—Gamble would make $3 million but he had to sign the deal within 10 minutes.

Frankly, he couldn't get the pen out of his pocket fast enough.

Thus, the nickname "Jesse James."

Tie One On

Second baseman Willie Randolph was placed on the disabled list one time leaving Gamble distraught.

It had nothing to do with Randolphs playing ability.

Gamble always had Randolph tie his ties when the team went out on road trips.

He'd get his just due later on, always trying to stir Randolph up with what the newspapers were saying about him.

If nothing was written, Gamble would make things up just to get a reaction.

What I Meant Was . . .

Casey Stengel wasn't the only Yankee who could mangle words and names. Gamble always called reliever Ray Fontenot (FON-ten-no) "Footnote."

When trying to refer to famed actor Efram Zimbalist Jr., Gamble called him "Epplin Zepplin Junior."

JOE GARAGIOLA

The Best Fiction Writer Couldn't Make This Up

Little Joe Garagiola and little Lawrence Peter Berra were best friends growing in an Italian neighborhood in St. Louis known as 'The Hill.'

So imagine the emotions stirring inside Joe G when he broadcast the 1964 World Series for NBC which pitted the St. Louis Cardinals against Yogi's Yankees.

"It was one of those moments if I would have dwelled upon it a little bit, I would have gotten goosebumps from it. He got fired right after that and lost it, I think, with the tying run at second base. We both thought he was gonna get rehired with a long-term contract."

Berra was gone to the Mets as a player/coach, just missing the collapse, as Garagiola was hired by the Yankees.

"That would have been neat but it was not to be. I was kind of glad because that was not a good team to manage."

Welcome to New York

After the 1964 World Series, Yogi Berra was not the only legend exiting the organization under bizarre circumstances. So did Mel Allen, replaced by Joe Garagiola.

"I was doing Game of the Week. A guy who was in charge of broadcasting for the club was the same guy I had worked for at NBC.

"Ralph Houk, who was now general manager, called me and asked if I would be interested in the Yankee job. I said, 'Absolutely. You'd be crazy not to be interested in it.' So he offered it to me and the next thing you know, I was broadcasting for the Yankees. I made it a point to say that there's no way you replace Mel Allen. He was perfect for the Yankees with that voice of his. He was just a tradition. For me to broadcast Yankee games it was great. There it was, Yankee Stadium, and I was working with Rizzuto, Jerry Coleman and Red Barber."

LOU GEHRIG

Young Lou

Lou Gehrig and Babe Ruth formed the most powerful pair of home run hitters in Major League history. Their Yankee paths would not cross until Gehrig arrived in 1923, but the two would be linked by reputation years earlier.

Gehrig led Commerce High School to the New York City scholastic championship during his senior year. As a result, the newly created *New York Daily News* sent the Commerce team out west to face Chicago city champion Lane Tech High School.

Commerce prevailed, 12-6, with Gehrig smashing a grand slam out of the park. Suddenly, Gehrig was tabbed, "The Babe Ruth of the High Schools."

It was a distinction Gehrig also earned while playing Collegiately for Columbia University. He hit seven home runs one season.

He Kept On Ticking

Lou Gehrig was nicknamed The Iron Horse for his incredible consecutive games playing streak of 2,130 games.

Lou Gehrig

Legend has the streak starting with manager Miller Huggins patting Gehrig on the back and telling him to replace Wally Pipp at first base, this taking place on June 1, 1925.

Actually, the day was correct but the first game of Gehrig's streak was a pinch-hitting appearance for rookie Pee Wee Wanninger.

The next day, Gehrig took over the first base duties from Pipp, who had suffered a bad beaning and was being phased out of the lineup.

It must also be noted that Gehrig was drilled in the forehead with a double-play throw in that same game, knocking him senseless. Asked if he wanted to be removed from the contest, Gehrig replied: " Hell, no! It's taken me three years to get into this game. It's going to take more than a crack on the head to get me out."

Fourteen years later, it was the debilitating effects of amyotrophic lateral sclerosis that forced Gehrig out of the lineup.

A side note: Wanninger actually bridged the gap between the record holders for consecutive games. A month earlier Wanninger had replaced Everett Scott, who owned the mark at 1,307 games.

Hey, That's My Job!

Wally Pipp's first brush with Gehrig took place in 1923.

Gehrig had just signed a pro contract with the Yankees—thus concluding an abbreviated college career with Columbia University—when Pipp was enlisted by a National League team to negotiate a contract with Gehrig.

Little did Pipp know at that time that Gehrig was already signed and would have Pipp's job inside of two years.

He Just Knew It

Hall of Famer Ty Cobb recognized Gehrig's greatness from the moment he donned the Yankee uniform.

"Lou Gehrig was the hustlinest ball player I ever saw, and I admired him for it," Cobb said in his Georgia accent.

"When I first saw him break in the lineup, as a rookie, I went and told him just that."

Plenty Tough

How tough was Lou Gehrig?

Consider, in his triple crown championship year of 1934, he fractured a toe and played on.

He also was knocked unconscious by a pitched ball, suffered a severe concussion and was still back in the lineup the next day.

X-rays showed he had broken every finger on both hands at some time in his career, 17 fractures in all—this, on top of all the other assorted injuries.

(Sort Of) Funny Stuff

Lou Gehrig and his wife, Eleanor, were very playful with one another.

They enjoyed roughhousing with one another. They'd wrestle and sometimes box.

One day Eleanor knocked Lou out with a single punch. After he shook off the blur, he burst out in laughter.

Lou's Little Helper?

Lou Gehrig did not abstain from alcohol altogether, but he rarely drank.

However, manager Miller Huggins noticed Gehrig was in the midst of a prolonged batting slump and decided to give his slugger $10 to go out on a bender.

JASON GIAMBI

The Wooing Was Alluring

Within days of their heartbreaking World Series defeat at the hands of the Arizona Diamondbacks, the Yankees began in earnest their wooing of Jason Giambi.

The 2000 American League MVP and runner-up to Ichiro Suzuki in 2001 received phone calls from Manager Joe Torre, Roger Clemens and Derek Jeter. Also recruited to sell him on the program was then-Mayor Rudy Giuliani who implored him to switch coasts because the Yankees were in need of another Italian star in the tradition of DiMaggio, Lazzeri, Crosetti, Berra and Rizzuto.

"Pop, It's Not Number 7, But We Got the Pinstripes"

So spoke Jason Giambi at his introductory press conference with the New York media.

Then he cried.

His father, John, a bank president in a town 30 miles from Los Angeles, grew up idolizing the Yankees in general and

Jason Giambi

Mickey Mantle and Yogi Berra in particular. He was a catcher with dreams of his own until a knee injury ended his baseball career in junior college.

So John did the next best thing. He passed that adoration on to his sons, Jason and Jeremy. As a reminder, Jason wore uniform number seven all his life until he signed with the A's as their second-round draft choice in 1992. There, Scott Brosius, soon to become a Yankee, had it. So he chose No. 16, the numerals adding to 7. In New York, it's No. 25, same reasoning.

"I'm just a normal kid off the street who had a dream to make this happen," Giambi said.

Part of that dream involves jewelry.

"I want to get a few of those things that Yogi uses for toe rings."

What else do you do with 10 World Series rings?

Missing the Mick

Years ago as a kid with the San Diego Padres, shortstop Ozzie Guillen got out of going to Instructional League by telling the ballclub his mother had died in Venezuela.

When he got there, his mother told him never to do that again.

In 1992, Jason Giambi, fresh off the U.S. Olympic Team in Barcelona, did heed the call of the A's and reported to Instructional League.

At the same time, his father and younger brother, Jeremy, traveled to an autograph show at the Pomona Fairgrounds in California to meet their idol, Mickey Mantle.

The Mick got out from behind the table he was sitting at to pose for pictures with the Giambis. People waiting in line behind them were getting antsy. Jason had missed the show.

Mickey Mantle died from liver cancer on August 13, 1995. Jason Giambi, in his rookie season, hit home runs each of the next three days.

Porch Power

Jason Giambi received a seven-year contract worth $120 million dollars. Not bad for a former 43rd round draft choice of the Milwaukee Brewers in 1989.

"I couldn't fathom all of the money that I had before," he said. "To have this situation is mind-boggling."

He did have one other request.

When asked about the possibility of Yankee Stadium aiding and abetting the lefthanded pull-hitter's ability to strike 50 homers, he said, "I'm not going to put that pressure on myself, but I was trying to get them to make it about 290 down the right-field line. I was trying to work with the dimensions."

Giambi on Broadway

At the Ed Sullivan Theater on Broadway, Jason Giambi visited the Late Show with David Letterman the day he signed.

With permission granted by Worldwide Pants Inc., from the home office in Wahoo, Nebraska, here are his top 10 reasons for wanting to play for the New York Yankees:

10.   I want to help the team fight the embarrassment of not winning a world championship in 14 months.

9.   When you say, "David Wells sent me," you get half-price drinks at Hooters.

8. Pinstripes are slimming.
7. After Chuck Knoblauch, people will think I have a great arm.
6. I hear Steinbrenner is a dream to work for.
5. Miss Cleo told me.
4. Diving into the stands for a foul ball and "accidentally" landing on Donald Trump's date.
3. Have you ever been to Oakland?
2. In New York, I'm closer to my favorite talk show host—Regis. And the number-one reason for wanting to play for the New York Yankees . . .
1. After the game, cruising bars with Giuliani and picking fights.

JAKE GIBBS

Get The Point?

Talk about the cure being worse than the ailment! Catcher Jake Gibbs got hit in the hand during spring training, and a trainer determined a hole had to be drilled through his fingernail to relieve the pressure.

The drill bit smoked as it bore through Gibbs' nail, but when it broke through Gibbs recoiled in pain.

The drill remained in the hole as he jumped around in agony.

You Know What I Mean!

Menu reading was not strength of Gibbs.

He ordered pie a la mode one time and then asked the waitress to put ice cream on it.

PAUL GIBSON

Walk a Mile in My Shoes

Paul Gibson's story with the Yankees is not about relief pitching but his memories of "Wade Boggs and his crazy superstitions."

He says that Boggs was very superstitious about his spikes. When he got hits, he would wear the same shoes.

"One particular night, we had a rain delay. He's walking around and his shoes are soaking wet. Everyone else is changing their shoes, socks and everything and he won't take his shoes off."

Naturally, the team was getting on him a little bit.

"After the rain delay ends, he comes in and throws the shoes in the garbage and puts a new pair of shoes on. I took the shoes out of the garbage and put them in my locker thinking they would be used for an auction someday, get him to sign them."

That's what he thought.

"Two innings later, he came back in and asked the clubhouse guy where the shoes were because he had struck out again and he wanted the old shoes back. So he retrieved the shoes from my locker and made the clubhouse guy take the shoelaces out and put new shoelaces in. That was the problem."

Obviously.

Hey, Let's Have a Catch...Now!!

And then Wade Boggs wanted to have a catch.

"He used to play catch in front of the dugout. A specific number of throws. He would grab the same guy every time. When I was there, it was Charlie Wonsowicz, the batting practice pitcher. No matter where he was, he had to be there at 7:13. Boggs wouldn't leave the dugout until the clock the clock ticked :13. He would make 13 or 14 tosses and the last one he would throw a knuckleball. So that night, I told Charlie when he gets ready to throw the last one, walk off. 'Don't let him throw you the ball. Just walk off the field.' Freaked out, Boggs was totally freaked out."

Boggs was hardly alone with his superstitions.

"Paul O'Neill was very similar. There was a young player who had just come up who was living up in Westchester. He wanted a ride to the ballpark. O'Neill was on a real hot streak. He was driving to the park by himself. The only person who could give this guy a ride from Westchester to the ballpark was O'Neill."

O'Neill refused.

"I think he had hit three home runs in four days or something like that. He refused him a ride to the ballpark because of that."

Lunchtime! Now!

Don't eat with Wade Boggs. Paul Gibson found out the hard way.

"We were in Oakland and I had had lunch with Wade at a restaurant. He got four hits that day. The next day he calls me in the room and he says, 'We're gonna go eat again.' I said, 'Well, I don't feel like eating this early.' He says, 'No, you have to eat with me.' I said, 'OK, I'll go with you.' He says to the maitre'd at the restaurant, 'We want that table over there.'"

It gets better.

"We get the same table we had before. He made me sit in the same seat that I sat in the day before. He made me order the same lunch that I had the day before. That was the kind of thing you dealt with with those two guys."

LEFTY GOMEZ

Hey, Batter!

What was the secret to Lefty Gomez' pitching success? "I talk 'em out of hits," Gomez said of the hitters.

Tension-breaker

Trips to the mound produced some of Gomez' best lines.

Catcher Bill Dickey visited one day and asked what they should throw Jimmie Foxx.

Said Gomez: "I don't want to throw him nothin'. Maybe he'll get tired of waitin' and leave." After loading the bases, manager Joe McCarthy took a visit and made the mistake of pointing out that very fact.

"I know they're loaded up," Gomez said. "Do you think I thought they gave me another infield?"

(Un)Desired Result

Talk about lanky—Gomez stood 6-foot-2 and weighed just 150 pounds.

General manager Ed Barrow suggested Gomez put on 20 pounds and then he'd make people forget about 41-game winner Jack Chesbro.

"I put on 20 pounds and almost made them forget Gomez," Gomez later quipped.

Dragging

As injuries and arm problems began to take their toll on the left-hander, Gomez said this of his fastball: "I'm throwing as hard as I ever did but the ball is just not getting there as fast."

Taking Credit

Gomez takes credit for making Joe DiMaggio the great outfielder that he was.

"I made him famous. They didn't know he could go back on a ball until he played behind me," Gomez joked.

JOHN GORDON

Sticking Up For a Guy

John Gordon had long held aspirations to broadcast major
league baseball. He thought he had made it, then he didn't,
then he did.

"I became very good friends with Gene Michael. He managed
the Columbus Clippers in '79. It's ironic. I was out of baseball
in 1981. I had been with the Clippers from 1977 through 1980.
Just through circumstances, I took a TV job in Columbus and
had kind of decided I wasn't gonna get to the big leagues so I
pursued this television opportunity.

That year, Gordon was calling the Liberty Bowl between
Ohio State and Navy in Memphis.

"On our way, I got a call from a guy in New York and I had
no idea who he was. He said there was an opening in the Yankee
booth and asked if I would be interested. I called Stick and he
wanted to know what they were offering. I went up to New York
and they made me an offer. When I went back to Columbus, I
called Stick and said they offered three years and good money.
At the time I questioned working for Steinbrenner, an issue, if
not the most important issue. Stick said, 'Hey, they offered you
a three-year deal. If it doesn't work out, it's three years you can
write off as an experience.' So we accepted the position and were
off and running in 1982."

John Gordon spent five seasons with the Yankees through 1986. He walked into a World Championship with the Minnesota Twins in 1987.

You-Know-Who Was on the Bridge
Scooter Scoots

"We had a game that went 17 innings. Scooter left like in the ninth like he always would. We struggled in the 15th, 16th and 17th innings. There were 2,000 people left in the stands. We were just trying to get through the ballgame. Steinbrenner was listening. It was one of the very few times that he ever really meddled. Usually, when the ballclub was going bad, that was when we had our best broadcasts because he never meddled. When the ballclub was going good, that was when we had our toughest broadcasts because he would get involved. In this instance, Frank Messer and I were on the air and Scooter was gone.

"It was tough. Steinbrenner called the broadcast director and wanted to know where Scooter was. He had crossed the bridge."

Hey, Scooter, this one is for you.

"The very next week we had another 17-inning game. Scooter stuck around. He didn't leave because the hammer had come down. We were doing the 17th inning like it was the seventh game of the World Series. You never heard a more exciting broadcast."

GOOSE GOSSAGE

Goose on Mo

"The first time that I saw him was in the Seattle playoffs in '95. I was watching it on TV at home in Colorado. He came into a bases-loaded situation and I looked at this kid get out of it without giving up a run. I'll tell you, right then I knew. I said, 'This kid is special'. But until he came up with the cutter, I think that he was starting to become hittable. Now, he has evolved into the game's best closer and has been just unhittable. That's not telling anybody any secrets. He has been flawless."

Then there is the emotional aspect of Rivera's appearance.

"There is nothing worse than being in the opposing dugout to watch a guy like that come into the ballgame and what a disheartening, sinking feeling it is."

He should know.

When I'm 64

Jesse Orosco, along with Terry Mulholland, whose performances may both date back to the first-ever boxscore in 1823, is reported to have told his wife he sees no reason why he cannot pitch in the major leagues until age 50. He receives support from Goose Gossage, who pitched until age 43.

"I'm 50 right now and I still throw batting practice to my son. My arm feels great. I don't see any reason why a relief pitcher being used correctly and sporadically in tough situations couldn't pitch until 50. The way the guys stay in shape today only helps their chances. Rick Honeycutt pitched until he was 43 or 44. If you're lefthanded, especially if you are lefthanded, you can come in and get one lefthander out. I don't put it beyond the realm that you could pitch until you're 50 years old."

Waiter, There's A Spy In The Booth

Major League Baseball has often used law enforcement agencies to get the message out to players about the ills of carousing, drugs and gambling.

One year baseball commissioner Bowie Kuhn made it known he had spies out in the bars and restaurants that players frequented.

One day, buddies Rich "Goose" Gossage and Graig Nettles decided they would try to find the spies and, in doing so, frequented a number of bars and eateries in the Milwaukee area. Their conclusion: Kuhn hired mooses.

They had seen one mounted in one bar and then another four hours later.

"That's the second moose we've seen today," Gossage said, figuring he found the spy.

This Way?

It's obvious wildlife and Gossage didn't mix well. Gossage took his wife out to dinner in Boston.

He cracked open the claw of a lobster, and one of the thorns on it went right into the fingernail of his index finger on his pitching hand.

Nettles used the opportunity to needle the pitcher the next day.

"Goose, cheeseburgers don't bite back! What are you trying to do?"

Gossage assured Nettles he was going back to the burgers.

RON GUIDRY

Ron Guidry proved to be the catalyst in the Yankees' 1978 championship run, but he almost never made it out of spring training in 1977.

Guidry was getting hit hard, prompting owner George Steinbrenner to go nuts.

Said the Boss to manager Billy Martin: "I got to get rid of him, he can't pitch, I got to get rid of that skinny kid. I'm telling you right now he can't pitch."

Fortunately, Martin and general manager Gabe Paul prevented Steinbrenner from pulling the trigger on a trade.

A year later, Guidry posted a 25-3 record and 1.74 earned run average, helped the Yankees to the American League East Division playoff victory at Boston's Fenway Park and won his lone start in the World Series triumph over the Los Angeles Dodgers.

Ron Guidry

John Habyan

The Steal Sign

Time for a tale from the bullpen. "One that stands out is that the Yankee bullpen has always been accused of tipping our hitters with signs from the opposing team. We're giving location. This day, we're playing Texas in Yankee Stadium."

There would be a line of guys in the bullpen who would sit up close to the wall on a bench. Here's how it worked.

"We would have one guy in a blue top, usually a jacket. Remember Carl Taylor? He did it most of the time. Everybody would wear white, so he would stick out. All we'd do is if he ate a sunflower seed, that meant the catcher was setting up in. If he didn't do anything, he was setting up away. We did this for a few series and some of the guys were having some pretty good success with it.

"Not everybody took advantage of the locale signs, but a few of the hitters did it because if the guy set up in, he pretty much knew it was a fastball.

"So it's this one afternoon against the Rangers. I think it's the third game of the series and we had been doing a pretty good job against them. All of a sudden, this little bat boy comes out to the bullpen, a little kid."

He had a note and it wasn't from his teacher.

"We read the note and it was from Bobby Valentine. It said, 'If that guy eats one more seed, the next guy's gonna catch it right in the dome.'"

That's when they told Carl Taylor to quit eating and shut it down.

"That's pretty good that he picked it up, though.

Paging Mr. Redass

John Habyan asks me, "Anybody guys giving you stories about guys getting picked off and snapping?"

Bring it on, I'd love that.

"When Stump Merrill was manager, we used to get a lot of work in the bullpen. The kiss of death was you were definitely in there if he gave you the day off. He did it to Steve Farr a lot.

"This one day I went out there and pitched the eighth. I come in the dugout and I thought for sure I was going out there for the ninth because I knew Steve had the day off. I knew he was hangin'."

No he wasn't.

"Mark Connor says, 'No, no, we're bringing The Beast in.' I'm like, OK, this should be good. So he calls up Beast and Beast comes in for the ninth inning and just gets his lunch. He gives up the lead. He thought he had the day off and he was tired."

And now, it's showtime.

"He comes in the dugout and goes up to the phone hanging on the wall. You know how it has a metal case around it and the front door swings open? He opens the case, takes the receiver and rips it right off. He hangs it back up and then with the line dangling out, then he closes the case again.

"He doesn't say a word and walks out of the dugout."

STEVE HAMILTON

P'tooey

Chewing tobacco has been a tradition—albeit a bad one—with baseball players for decades. Pitcher Steve Hamilton not only chewed at the ballpark, he chewed everywhere. Even his living room had a spittoon in the middle of it.

One night while pitching in Kansas City, Hamilton accidentally swallowed his chaw. He turned around and threw up all over the back of the pitching mound.

RON HASSEY

Meet the Babe

Ruth wasn't the only lefthanded hitter the Yankees called "Babe." "The name came about when we were playing in Baltimore. Butch Wynegar got hurt and I went into the ballgame that night and proceeded to go 0-for-4. The next night I got another start and I hit two home runs. Earl Weaver commented in the paper, "Who does Hassey think he is, Babe Ruth?" That kind of stuck with me.

Ironic that it happened in the city where the Babe, the original, was born and raised.

Hello, Goodbye, Hello, Goodbye, Hello, Goodbye

Read any good resumes lately of any players traded twice by the same team to the same team?

"It started when I was traded from the Cubs to the Yankees in '85. At the end of the season, I was traded to the Chicago White Sox. Just before spring training started, I got traded back to the Yankees. Then in the middle of the '86 season, I was traded back to the White Sox. During that time I was injured.

I had a bad knee. There, I finished out the season. After the '87 season, I think it was, I became a free agent and almost signed back with the Yankees. Instead, I went with the Oakland As."

All the movement did not sit well with Hassey.

"It kind of was very frustrating because I really enjoyed playing in New York. I finally found a place that I really liked. I liked the big-city atmosphere. The fans of New York were outstanding to me. I had a good year there. I had a pretty good season in '85 and I was really looking forward to the '86 season. Then I went back and forth and when it happened again in the middle of the season, the second time was very frustrating. There was no time to think about it."

TOMMY HENRICH

Big Moments

Tommy Henrich was in awe of the Yankees when he joined them in 1937. It's not as though Henrich didn't fit in—he played 11 seasons with the Yankees and produced some of the biggest plays in World Series history.

He produced the series-winning hit in 1947 against Brooklyn.

Two years later his home run gave Allie Reynolds a 1-0 win over Don Newcombe in the opener.

In 1941, it was Henrich who swung and missed a pitch that was misplayed by Brooklyn catcher Mickey Owens. "When I saw that little jackrabbit bouncing, I said, 'Let's go.'"

The Yankees went on to win that game and the series.

And The Difference Is . . .

"Catching a fly ball is a pleasure. But knowing what to do with it after you catch it is a business."

—Tommy Henrich

FRANK HOWARD

In the opening game of the 1963 World Series, playing in the old Yankee Stadium with the field dimensions that stretched northward to Yonkers, 6-7, 275-pound Frank Howard of the Los Angeles Dodgers batted against Whitey Ford.

"I hit a line-drive off the monuments. For most guys, it would be a stand-up triple or possible inside-the-park home-run. For me, it was a head-first slide just to get a double out of it."

Legend has it that Tony Kubek, playing shortstop, jumped for the ball.

"I didn't see him jump for it. You know, in World Series play, you're psychologically so high, especially in the first game. I knew it had a chance to go in the gap for extra bases."

It makes for a better story that Howard never saw if Kubek jumped.

Hondo and Mickey

"You know, it's kind of a funny thing in our business. As we get a little bit older and look back on our careers, our minds expand. The balls keep going further and going there more often."

Frank said he talked to Mickey Mantle right before he passed away.

"He asked me a question: 'How many times did you strike out?' And I said, 'About fourteen hundred and something.'

"He said, 'Well, I got you beat. It's about seventeen hundred. How many times did you walk?'

"I said, 'Probably about fifteen hundred times.' He said, 'I got you beat, about eighteen hundred times.'

"He says, 'That's about 6,000 at-bats. Do you realize that based on a 600 at-bat year for 10 years, we didn't do much on a baseball field?' That put it in its proper prospective."

Welcome to Baseball's Golden Age

Frank Howard says he doesn't want to detract from the "great things these young people are doing today.

"I've seen Stargell, I've seen McCovey, I've seen Frankie Robinson, I've seen Killebrew. I've seen guys hit baseballs unbelievable distances. But you get the mighty McGwire. He has consistently hit the ball further than anybody that's ever played this game, including Ruth."

Howard asked Killebrew if he ever hit 50 home runs in a season.

"Harmon told me, 'No, Frank, I hit 49 twice.' I said, 'Can you imagine a guy hitting 70 or more home runs?' He said, 'Not in my wildest dreams.'

"That's 21 home runs more than one of the greatest power hitters and Hall of Famers that ever lived.

"People say to me, 'Well, the ball's juiced, the pitching's thinner, the ballparks are small.' Today's guys with that size and that strength are making them play smaller.

"I don't care. You hit 70 or 73 home runs, that has got to be recognized. To sit back and say, 'That's the way it used to be,' that's a bunch of bull. They talk about the good old days. Well, the good old days are today."

He Might Have Won the Player of the Week Award

Playing for Washington in 1968, over the course of just one week, Frank Howard struck 10 home runs. In just 20 at-bats.

"Those 10 home runs were hit off of Detroit, Boston, Cleveland and then Detroit."

Retaliation was never on order.

"I thought after a while someone might crease me, but it never happened."

Frank says this major league record is no big deal.

"If you can't hit 10 home runs in a week, you shouldn't be playing in that league.

"Somebody once asked me, 'Did you really hit a ball over the left field roof at Tiger Stadium?'

"I said, 'If you can't hit one over that roof, you shouldn't be playing in this league.'

And then Frank Howard added, "That's why they call it the big leagues. The thrill of competing against the world's greatest baseball players, I don't think there's anything that beats it."

STEVE HOWE

Number 57 in Your Program

From the beginning of his career until the end, Steve Howe wore uniform number 57. A cut number. "When I went to spring training in 1980, I told my wife and everyone that I got invited to early spring camp. I said I was going there to make the club. When I got down there, that was what they gave the batting practice pitchers and rookies and stuff."

Howe was true to his word.

"When I made the club, they said, 'OK, you get a good new number now, kid.' I said, 'For what? A number doesn't make the athlete. The athlete makes the number. They'll remember it one way or another.' And they did."

A Dream Fulfilled

Steve Howe was on the Stadium mound long before he became a Yankee in 1991. Ten years earlier, he was busy nailing down the final outs in the Dodgers' six-game victory in the 1981 World Series.

"The biggest thing for me personally as an athlete was to be able to go to the next level. For me to be involved in two saves and one win in the World Series not only was special but that it came against the New York Yankees. The New York Yankees are an icon on sports. They are 'the' sports franchise. They have the oldest tradition with Scooter, Thurman Munson, Reggie Jackson, Mickey, Billy, all those people, you automatically go, 'Yankees.' To beat them was even bigger because we weren't supposed to. We were the kids."

Every kid dreams of the moment Howe experienced.

"For me, it's the pinnacle for an athlete is to win a World Championship. Great, great, great players who I respect very much, Mr. Cub, Ernie Banks, all those guys never got a World Championship. And they deserved it. There's only one thing in my life that I ever experienced that was any higher than that moment. That was when my children were born healthy."

Beating the Door Down

It took persistence for Steve Howe to become a Yankee.

"Peter Ueberroth had basically blacklisted me when he was Commissioner. So I went to Japan and to Mexico. I had had an arm surgery and I was playing winter ball. I had taken my family down there during the Gulf War. We couldn't come home because of that. When I finally did, my agent, Dick Moss, was talking to Gene Michael, who was the Yankee GM."

Howe says Michael promised his agent a tryout. "We checked with scouts and he really wasn't throwing that well," Michael reportedly said.

"That's how it always goes. Then all of sudden he went cold on us. He wouldn't return Dick's phone calls and spring training had already started. I had put all my eggs in one basket, to go with the Yankees."

And because he had, Howe took matters into his own hands.

"Cindy and I took money we did not have, bought plane tickets to fly down to Fort Lauderdale and went up to Gene's door. When Dick Moss walked in, Gene came out and Dick said, 'We're here.' And Gene said, 'What are you doing here?' And Dick said, 'You were gonna give Steve a shot.' Howe says Gene said, 'I never said that. Get in my office.' They went in the office and Cindy and I stood outside the office. We took a 100% chance. About twenty minutes later, Stick says, 'You have your cleats and your glove with you?' I said, 'Yep.' He said, 'Come on out and throw.' Once he saw me, and I was throwing 94 miles per hour, he said, 'Come back again tomorrow. Can you do that again?'

Howe told Michael he was a little bit stiff.

"I came back the next day and threw harder. I signed that day. I was never invited. I just showed up."

Steve Howe earned a minor league contract and began the 1991 season in Triple-A Columbus where he recorded five saves. He was promoted in May and immediately became the big club's most effective reliever, pitching to a 1.68 ERA.

Loaded for Bear

In 1996, just after his release from the Yankees brought his career to an end, Steve Howe thought he was on his way home to Montana. Instead, he was arrested at JFK Airport and charged with carrying a concealed handgun in a carry-on bag aboard a plane. Howe says he did no such thing.

"The gun wasn't mine. It was never on a carry-on. No one knows that the wife of a friend of mine who is a policeman in New York and my wife packed that gun. It was in my wife's locked suitcase. I had no knowledge it was even there. They knew it was me and they arrested me. So once again, I ate it. I'm a lot more stand-up guy than people think."

Kathy

Steve Howe lost his beloved sister to cancer. She was 39.

"It's still hard to talk about because I miss her. She was a little over 13 months younger than me. She is the only person in my life I never had an argument with. She was always my fragile little sister and I always tried to take care of her. We were joined at the hip. What she meant to me was no judgment and unselfish love. I had to go and be with her and watch someone who was as precious to me as life itself die. The helplessness that I felt made me a ten-times better person because you know what, we're not here to like everybody and we're not here to be treated well by everybody. But we can still make a difference by liking everybody who is likable. And we can make a huge difference by treating people the way we wanted to be treated. And that is the way my sister was."

MILLER HUGGINS

Do As I Say...

Miller Huggins not only managed some of the top players of all time, but he also had to sit on them as the Yankees were a raucous and partying bunch.

Shortstop Mark Koenig liked to tell the story about how Huggins would lecture his club on the ills of drinking too much, especially after losses.

Sometimes the players listened, most times they did not.

One early morning, at about 4 a.m., Huggins caught one of his pitchers breaking curfew. The hurler had a blonde on one arm and a red head on the other.

"Good morning, son," said the manager.

"Hi-yah, Hug!" replied the pitcher.

Later that same day, Huggins reamed his pitcher out for carousing and getting plastered in public. The manager threatened a fine the next time it happened, and the pitcher understood.

However, on the way out of Huggins' office, the player turned and asked who turned him in.

REGGIE JACKSON

Incredibly Edible

Reggie Jackson hit 156 home runs as a New York Yankee, 12 in postseason play. What's his recipe for success? Rice and greens.

"With greens and rice, I don't leave 'em (hits) on the warning track," Jackson once said.

"The Straw"

Reggie Jackson got off on the wrong foot when he arrived in New York in 1977.

Not only were players jealous of his five-year, $2.9 million deal, but he bucked ranks by declaring himself to *Sport* magazine that he was "the straw that stirs the drink."

That interview infuriated catcher Thurman Munson. Of the team captain, Jackson said, "Munson thinks he can be the straw that stirs the drink, but he can only stir it bad."

When Jackson told Munson some of the quotes were taken out of context, all Munson could say was, "For four pages?"

Reggie Jackson

How About Some Onions?

"There isn't enough mustard to cover that hot dog," former Oakland A's teammate Darold Knowles said of Jackson.

DEREK JETER

A Dream Comes True

Playing ball for the New York Yankees is what Derek Jeter dreamed about while growing up nearby in New Jersey. Once in a while his grandmother would treat him to bleacher tickets. While he admired the likes of Don Mattingly, Willie Randolph and Dave Winfield, he always pictured himself playing shortstop.

Reality arrived in 1996, a year in which the rookie would start at shortstop during the World Series.

"This is what you've always thought about," Jeter said at the dawn of a Fall Classic showdown with the Atlanta Braves.

"From the time you start playing ball, you think about playing in the World Series. And if you've ever been inside Yankee Stadium, you think about playing here."

Star-crossed

When stars cross, sparks are bound to follow.

Joe DiMaggio had Hollywood actress Marilyn Monroe. Derek Jeter had superstar singer Mariah Carey. Jeter dated the singer during the 1998 season but their romance broke up.

Derek Jeter

Hi, Derek (Insert Giggle Here)!

A quick bat, a solid glove and a strong arm can make you an All-Star, but youth and good looks will get you fan mail from adoring women.

Derek Jeter is a leader in the Yankee clubhouse for letters and remains the player most in demand among single women in New York.

"I've been here 42 years and I've never see girls go fanatical about a ballplayer like this," said Yankee Stadium vendor Kenneth Spinner.

Doubling Up

Winning the World Series and American League rookie of the year honor in the same year was a dream come true for 22-year-old Derek Jeter in 1996.

How long did he celebrate the championship? One month, and then it was back to work at Yankees camp in Tampa, Florida, fielding grounders and adding 15 pounds to his frame.

When teammate Mariano Duncan received a phone call from Jeter in Tampa, he wondered why his fellow infielder was in camp so early.

"What he's showing everybody," Duncan said, "is he wants to get better and better."

True, Jeter followed up his .314 first season with a .291 average as a sophomore. But by his third season, Jeter established a new home run record for Yankee shortstops with 19 in 1998.

TOMMY JOHN

On Tommy John Surgery

Tommy John hasn't pitched since 1989 and yet, he sees his name in the paper with alarming regularity. And it alarms him.

"Never in my wildest dreams did I think that it was going to happen all these times when I had it done back in '74. I just thought I was the unlucky guy who had a misfortune. The problem that I see is why are all these guys having it?"

John thinks the fault lies with everyone in baseball, from the coaches in high school and college and strength coaches.

"Dr. Andrews has done over 1,000 now. Dr. Jobe has done well over 1,000 and there are probably two or three thousand other doctors out there that are doing the same surgery numerous times. So we have to be doing something wrong as to why these kids are having it. Dr. Andrews just operated on a kid 15 years old. He said that should never, ever, ever, ever happen."

John's personal feeling is these kids have been sold a bill of goods that they can become better pitchers if they go in the weight room and begin lifting.

"You become a better pitcher by pitching, by throwing the ball. And I think, personally, we've got to get back to think things the way they used to be done. I realize the methods and

Tommy John

the training are much better. But something's wrong when all these guys are having Tommy John surgery.

"It's nice to see your name out there and you know that the surgery is bringing guys off the scrap heap but there's a reason why they're having to have the surgery and I think something is wrong in the training programs."

9/11

Through sheer coincidence, Tommy John literally had a bird's eye view of the tragedy at the World Trade Center.

"I was landing at LaGuardia Airport. We were on final approach. The pilot informed us that both towers were on fire. In fact, my wife's got a picture of the World Trade Center burning from the window of the airplane as we were making a right-hand turn going up the East River."

Nobody on board knew what had happened.

"I thought there was a grease fire or something in the restaurant of one of the buildings. And then when we saw the smoke billowing, I thought there had been a gas explosion or something. We had a friend of ours who worked down there on Wall Street and we couldn't get through on the phone. Then, we called his wife and she told us what happened. My wife told others about the turn of events and cellphones started coming out all over the place."

CLIFF JOHNSON

Buckle Your Seatbelts, It's Going to Be a Bumpy Ride

Cliff Johnson was being dealt to a great 1977 club, the New York Yankees. "It was really horrible the way the Astros traded me. They traded me getaway night, which was also the trading deadline. That night we had a game in the Astrodome against the Mets. After the game, we were gonna open up a seven-game road swing with three games in New York and four games in Montreal. They don't tell me before our charter leaves. They tell me when we're about 18,000 feet in the air. Bob Lillis, who was a coach, comes back to tell me that the skipper wants to see me up front. I go up to see what he wants and Bill Virdon looks through these horn-rimmed glasses with this look on his face and tells me that I'm a Yankee now."

In trading him in the manner in which they did, Johnson said that nullified his 72-hour period to report.

"I spent the night in the hotel with the Astros but I was going to the opposite side of town. I was kind of in awe when I joined the Yankees. When Gabe Paul picked me up at the hotel that morning after we had breakfast, we took a cab up to Yankee Stadium. I had never been there before. I'm a kid off the west side of San Antonio. I had never been to the Bronx. I met Billy Martin for the first time. Billy was very cordial and warm and his old cunning self when he needed to be. And here was there 650-pound gorilla sitting behind this large, gorgeous desk by the name of George Steinbrenner. He was also very cordial and nice. One of the first things he asked me was if I had my bats. I told them I was sure they went over at Shea Stadium. He sent somebody over to get my bats. He asked me what size shoes I wore. He had shoes brought in. He's sitting behind this desk pressing buttons. I'm going, wow, this guy is like the President of the United States or something."

Balms Away

"What Sparky Lyle pulled on Yogi was a classic. Every night after a ballgame was over, Yogi would use Sparky's toothpaste. Knowing Count the way he was, and he was a great prankster anyway, he said he was gonna get even with Yogi. He took some of that analgesic balm and put it into the tube of toothpaste. I think that stopped Yogi from borrowing Sparky's toothpaste."

JAY JOHNSTONE

J ay Johnstone received a World Series ring with the 1978 Yankees. But he would never, ever confuse their collective personality with the champions next year, the 'We Are Familee' Pittsburgh Pirates.

"That was a team that went against the grain in what you'd want in a team as far as relationships go. The '78 team was a bunch of individuals. There were a lot of cliques on that team. A lot of guys would spar back and forth and you sometimes didn't know if it was for fun or if it was for real. There were a lot of guys on that team that didn't like each other. I swear if the game were to end and you would be walking across the street and somebody got hit by a bus, most of the guys would keep going and leave you there. But once they put on the Yankee uniform and walked across the white line, it was a whole different group of guys. For whatever it was on that field, when they put on the uniform that said 'Yankees', they came together. As soon as they went on the other side of the line and got into the clubhouse, they went back to being themselves again. I've never seen anything like it in my whole life."

Payback

Jay Johnstone played sparingly for the Yankees in 1979 before being dealt on the old June 15 deadline in the big Dave

Wehrmeister trade. He played out his option that season with the Pods and signed with the Dodgers. That set the stage for a pivotal at-bat against the Yankees in the 1981 World Series.

The Dodgers lost the first two games in New York. In Game Three on Friday night, Fernando Valenzuela staggered to victory, allowing 17 baserunners. The following afternoon, the Dodgers trailed 6-4 when Johnstone pinch-hit in the sixth inning.

Here is Jay Johnstone as Babe Ruth in 1932 at Wrigley Field.

"The irony of it is I had predicted it and showed the writers in batting practice if I got into the game today this is what I was going to do: hit a home run. They said, 'Yeah, right.'"

Johnstone told an audience of about 20 writers how he was going to do it.

"I said, 'Here's what I'm gonna do. I'm gonna shorten up my stance just a little bit and shorten my stride. Instead of taking my normal six-inch stride, I'm gonna go up and down real fast so I can get that bat head out and be quick.' Then I proceeded to hit, like, five or six balls out of the ballpark in batting practice. Then I told them, 'If Gossage comes in and throws me a fastball, it's gonna be up in the strike zone, I'm gonna raise my hands a little bit so my hands are shoulder high.' And they're still going, 'Yeah, right, right.'"

Everyone was now on notice.

"I got in the game early, in the sixth inning, and Ron Davis was pitching. But he threw the ball just as hard as Gossage. He threw me that fastball right out over the plate and I did exactly as I said."

The homer tied the game 6-6 and the Dodgers eventually won. The writers came down after the game.

"They couldn't believe it. Of course, I know it's one of those things where the chances of me doing that were slim and none. I got the opportunity and it just happened to work out my way and I became the hero for that."

STEVE KARSAY

Dreams Do Come True

I n his senior year at Christ the King High School in Queens, Steve Karsay played sandlot ball that summer for the Long Island Tigers.

Can you imagine being in high school and playing in Yankee Stadium?

"It was great being in Yankee Stadium for the first time and pitching off the mound. Going in there as a kid was a fun time. It's hard to explain, to go out to Monument Park to warm up in the Yankee bullpen to pitch on the field."

Karsay had been in the Stadium but had been unable to pitch.

"I had pitched two days before to get us to the championship game at Yankee Stadium. So I played first base. We ended up losing but it was still a thrill to be on the field and to play a seven-inning game there."

But it was still frustrating not being able to pitch.

"It was something that I wanted to do. I told my coach I was able to pitch an inning or two if he needed me. But that day was draft day and I actually got drafted on the day we played in Yankee Stadium. So even though we lost, it was still a great day for me."

Karsay was drafted 22nd overall in the 1990 draft by Toronto. A dozen years later, he is being introduced to the

New York media in Yankee Stadium when GM Brian Cashman demonstrates a keen memory.

"He told me that he remembered seeing me play as a high school player at a tryout. I thought that was kind of neat that he could remember that far back and still know who exactly I was today."

Paying Admission

Playing for the Yankees in 2002 was Steve Karsay's fifth incarnation inside Yankee Stadium: as a child watching from the stands for the first time, with Christ the King, with the Long Island Tigers, as an opposition player and now pitching for the home team. He vividly remembers stage one.

"I wasn't able to get there as often as to Shea Stadium which was closer to my house. But to go to Yankee Stadium and to sit in the stands and knowing the guys who played there, Mickey Mantle, Joe DiMaggio, Babe Ruth, to have the aura of the stadium and the feeling of a baseball game with the New York Yankees in the pinstripes was special. I always wanted to go to Yankee games growing up. I relished every game I was able to go to there. I was 10 years old when I went there for the first time and they were playing the Boston Red Sox. I was in awe of what was around me and all the people that were there and what the Stadium meant."

Steve Karsay

STEVE KEMP

Merge Ahead

One of the most severe fielding accidents in Yankee history was the result of two pieces of cotton. In a game at Toronto's Exhibition Stadium, a pop fly was lifted into short right-center field. Second baseman Willie Randolph was running back on the ball while outfielders Jerry Mumphrey and Steve Kemp rushed in. Mumphrey called for the ball, only Randolph couldn't hear over the wind and Kemp couldn't hear because of the cotton balls he placed in his ears to ward off the frosty effect of the wind.

Randolph got the palm of his glove on the ball before Kemp slammed into him and then stepped on Mumphrey's foot. The ball fell loose, setting up a gamewinning rally for the Blue Jays.

Mumphrey suffered a broken toe and Kemp severely banged up his shoulder.

What The Heck

Steve Kemp always hustled in whatever he did. Kemp once scored from first base on a two-out popout that was heading foul into the stands only to have the wind take the ball back in and deposit it on the line.

Just another day, he said.

"With two outs I had nothing else to do, so I figured I might as well."

CLYDE KING

DH, You're the One

In 2002, Clyde King began his 27th year in the Yankee
organization. How many people can boast of that?

"I wish everybody knew George Steinbrenner like I know
him. His compassion for people that work for him."

You're kidding?

"No. He's tough sometimes, but he's never really mean to
you. He may say something that appears to be mean at the time
but he'll come back later and make things better. He's just been
a wonderful person to work for. It hasn't always been easy working for him but it hasn't always been difficult working for him,
either. I would say the majority of the time it has been absolutely
fabulous. You know, as you go through the valley with George
Steinbrenner, the valley is not very deep. You don't stay in it very
long. You're back on the mountaintop soon. The thing about
Mr. Steinbrenner is he never expects any of us to do anything he
wouldn't do. I never had a problem putting in hours for him."

One Score Ago

In 1982, George Steinbrenner asked Clyde King, who
managed Atlanta and San Francisco previously, to leave the

front office and replace Gene Michael as manager. This was one of those schizophrenic years. Michael had replaced Bob Lemon.

"I really was not gung-ho managing. I didn't want to manage that year where the players were difficult to discipline. Mr. Steinbrenner is a disciplinarian, just like I am. I think that's one reason we got along. I wanted players to be on time and if they messed up, I wanted to be able to fine them. At that time, you couldn't fine a player more than $500 without going to arbitration, terrible things like that."

King enjoyed the work he was doing upstairs.

"I was doing advance scouting ahead of the team, looking at players we were interested in. When I went back down there, though, I enjoyed it. Several people said I changed the attitude of the team. We had a lot of guys hurt. That was the reason it was going poorly for Gene Michael. We just weren't up to par."

Clyde King won 29 games and lost 33 as Yankee manager. The club finished fifth, 79-83, 16 games behind division-leading Milwaukee.

Ron Kittle

Pay Attention!!

"Everybody's dream is to be a New York Yankee. Everybody's probably told you that." That from Ron Kittle. He was to be A.L. Rookie of the Year with the Chicago White Sox, soaking up the aura that is Yankee Stadium.

"My first appearance in New York, I was in leftfield while we were taking batting practice. The Thurman Munson video came up on the big screen."

Kittle made the mistake of turning away.

"I was hit with a line-drive smack in the side of the head. And not one time did I flinch or move because I was so engrossed in what I was watching. When you're in an arena like that, you just don't feel any pain. And it was downhill after that."

Attitude Problems

If he had to do it over again, Ron Kittle would have adopted a different attitude when the White Sox traded him to the Yankees.

"I did things the wrong way. I was very upset with the White Sox when I got traded over there. Instead of putting a positive spin on it and saying the New York Yankees needed me to help them out, I wasn't old enough at the time to understand that."

When Kittle did report to the Yankee locker room, he made an unforgettable impression by committing blasphemy.

"Thurman Munson's locker is not used. I walk in and everybody knew I had a sense of humor. I walked over there and threw my gear into Thurman's locker and said, 'Who the hell is this Munson fella?'"

The shrine had been breached.

"Everybody just got real quiet in the locker room."

Retribution

Ron Kittle never imagined home runs would cost him money.

"When I was with the White Sox, I hit a home run against Bob Shirley and another against Tim Stoddard in the same game.

Then Kittle was traded to the Yankees.

"It's about two-and-a-half-weeks later and we have a kangaroo court. I was fined $250 each for hitting home runs against my teammates."

DAVE LAPOINT

Who Exactly is the Home Team?

D ave LaPoint was on the mound in Yankee Stadium at the moment it was announced that George Steinbrenner was banished from baseball by Commissioner Fay Vincent.

"We were playing Detroit. You know that everybody in the Stadium has their radio on. At that time, they all hated George and couldn't wait to hear something bad about him. I gave up a two-run home run to Cecil Fielder going the opposite direction and as the ball goes over the fence, the crowd let out with this tremendous roar."

LaPoint gave up his share of home runs, but never once did he experience a post-homer reaction like this.

"They're all celebrating. From the mound, it looks like they're gonna charge the field. Everybody's running down the aisles to get to the front row. It was at that very moment that they announced that George had been suspended and all the fans were cheering."

LaPoint said it was a terrible feeling.

"I don't know how many people were there that night but it was bad being on the mound. The reaction just towards one guy was unbelievable. At that time, you just felt bad for George. There they were in his house and they're acting like that."

DON LARSEN

El Perfecto

Twenty-seven batters, 27 outs. A perfect game. It is a feat rarely accomplished by any pitcher and, until the afternoon of October 8, 1956, had not been performed on a stage as large as the World Series.

Larsen altered his pitching style as the season progressed, making it more difficult for batters to pick up what he was doing.

By ridding himself of a windup motion, batters had a tough time spotting the different grips he used for his pitches.

The National League champion Brooklyn Dodgers, which faced Larsen in Game Five that day, with the series knotted up at two games apiece, certainly hadn't faced Larsen much at all.

As the game moved into its later innings, Larsen tempted the baseball gods. Standing next to Mickey Mantle, Larsen leaned over and said, "Wouldn't it be something if I pitched two more innings with a no-hitter?"

The Mick just walked away.

"We all got the same idea about that time and cleared away from Don," Mantle said. "Larsen wasn't nervous, but the rest of us were."

The last batter was pinch-hitter Dale Mitchell, a spray hitter. With a 1-2 count, Larsen got Mitchell looking as umpire Babe Pinelli rang him up on strikes.

Don Larsen

Catcher Yogi Berra ran out to meet Larsen between home plate and the mound, leaping into his pitcher's arms.

Two Of A Kind

Don Larsen and David Wells are two of only three New York Yankees to pitch perfect games.

Larsen performed his in the 1956 World Series against the Brooklyn Dodgers. Wells tossed his in May 1998 against the Minnesota Twins.

What is another link between the two? Both graduated from the same high school, Point Loma in San Diego.

PHIL LINZ

Maestro, If You Please, Do You Know 'Play Me or Keep Me?'

It was a variation on a popular theme. "I said it to Ralph Houk. It broke up the bus. I'm glad he got a kick out of it. Joe Garagiola was announcing for us at the time and he came up with the idea. We were in the back of the bus as usual, cutting up, making jokes. I guess I got 4-for-5 one day. I was hot. I was getting two hits, three hits, four hits. As soon as I went 0-for-3, I was right back on the bench. Of course, they kept me. They didn't play me. That was the worst part."

Mr. Laffs

No listing of every hot nightspot in Manhattan over the last 40 years would be complete without this one.

"We lived at the Loews Midtown on 48th and 8th Avenue. I was living there with Bud Daley, a lefthanded junkball pitcher. I had a '64 T-Bird. They let us stay there for $7 a day. We had lived in the Bronx where we were paying $6 a day. Bob Tisch set us up, told us to come downtown for a dollar more a day. We had a swimming pool and free parking for the T-Bird. Around

Phil Linz

three o'clock, we'd drive up 8th Avenue and go to the St. Moritz, double park and then go up and see Mickey. We'd wait for him to get ready and then we'd go through Central Park to go to the ballpark."

Then came the fateful elevator ride.

"I meet this stewardess and get her number. We're going up to Boston for a weekend series. When we get back, I give her a call. She lives at 65th Street and First Avenue. We're in a cab and she says, "You know, there's no guys in this building. There's nothing but girls, all airline stewardesses. There's like about 50 guys and 300 stewardesses." The next day, we saw the superintendent of her building and signed a lease for an apartment."

Think that's lucky? Get this.

"Bob Anderson was my next door neighbor. He played left halfback at West Point and then for the Giants. He had just gotten out of football after hurting his knee. The superintendent asked if we wanted to become partners and would be interested in opening up a club inside an empty store on First Avenue. Why not? We'll have some fun and do it for laughs."

Ralph Houk didn't think it was so funny.

"He called me in the office during the season and said, 'I hear you're opening a place. We don't think it's a good idea.' I said, 'Why not?'

"He says, 'Well, you're playing here in New York and it's gonna distract you from playing.' I said, 'Well it's too late now. I already have my money into it.'"

Right before the club opening in December, 1965, Phil Linz was traded to Philadelphia for Ruben Amaro.

"I'm pretty sure that was one of the reasons. Of course, I only hit .207 that season. I was just pretty lucky it was close."

Here, Catch

Phil Linz, a native of Baltimore, invites his parents to Memorial Stadium to see him play for the Yankees. He will never, ever forget this.

"It is June 4, 1963, and I'm at bat. I hit a foul ball into the stands. My father catches it."

This made the Baltimore papers.

"My father sends a postcard to that show in New York 'I've Got a Secret.' Three weeks later, around World Series time, my parents come up from Baltimore. They put them up in a hotel and put them on the show. The celebrities guessed it."

Not Doing it For the Money

Phil Linz was out of baseball at 29.

"I was pretty bored. I wasn't making any money either, so that was another reason. After the 1964 season and the harmonica thing, the Yankees sent me a contract for $20,200. The $200 was for music lessons. That was in my contract. Actually, they were repaying my fine that I got that summer. I got fined $250 by Yogi."

Time for trivia. Can you imagine who was the youngest ex-player ever invited to Old Timers Day at Yankee Stadium?

"It was a record. I wasn't shocked, I was embarrassed big time. I was too embarrassed to go. I never showed up there, no way, no way. I was younger than most of the players on the current team. I didn't go back for years."

This is Easy

Phil Linz was 1-for-3 in the 1963 World Series against the Dodgers. The '1' was against Koufax. Of course.

"It was my first time at bat. First pitch fastball hit one bounce between third and short that went through. It looked to me like he was so easy to hit."

Oh, you're the guy.

"He didn't have any deception and came right over the top. The ball was nice and white and came right out of his hand. It looked so easy.

"I was a good fastball hitter, a good high fastball hitter. I threw the bat head out and it went through the infield."

Time to hit again.

"The next time at bat, he threw me some fastballs that I could hardly see. It was like jet propulsion. It looked the same to me. The ball was released out of his hand and I saw it real well. Here it comes and then it would just explode and blew right past me. It's hard to get your hands started. Incredible."

What'd He Say?

Clubhouses and team buses are loose places after a victory, but following losses sometimes it's best not to say a word.

In August 1964, the Yankees were swept in four games by the Chicago White Sox at Comiskey Park. While a team bus full of players, coaches and assigned media made its way to O'Hare International Airport, utility infielder Phil Linz broke out a harmonica he had just purchased.

Linz had no lessons on how to play and was trying to follow some scripted instructions on how to play the song "Mary Had a Little Lamb."

The off-key rendition irritated manager Yogi Berra, who was sitting in the front seat of the bus still stewing over the four losses.

The skipper had said something that Linz couldn't hear, so Mickey Mantle—never one to pass up a good joke opportunity—relayed to Linz that he should play louder.

Next thing anyone knew, Berra stormed to the back of the bus.

"Hey, Linz. Go stick that harmonica up your ass," Berra said.

Linz was stunned at first and then threw the harmonica at Berra, who promptly threw it back at Linz. However, Yogi's throw was off target and the harmonica hit first baseman Joe Pepitone in the knee. Playing it up, Pepitone pleaded for a medic.

Linz apologized to Berra the next day, but the manager still fined him $250.

After the story hit the news wires, executives from the Hoehner Harmonica Co. contacted Linz and offered him $5,000 to endorse their product.

As it turned out, the Yankees would be playing a winning tune a month later, winning the American League pennant by one game over the same Chicago White Sox.

DON LOCK

Maybe They Won't Notice

S pring training cuts are the worst to handle. The notices come in the form of red tags or notes on a locker or a whisper from a messenger.

Clubhouse manager Pete Sheehy was the bearer of bad news for many Yankee hopefuls.

One year, minor league outfielder Don Lock tried his best to avoid being declared dead, a term players use for being cut. He crossed out his name atop his locker and then barricaded himself in the locker with sweatshirts, gloves and shoes.

Pretending his bat was a rifle, Lock would "fire" at anyone who approached his little foxhole.

In the end, Sheehy managed to get his message across.

HECTOR LOPEZ

The 1961 Yankees, immortalized in books and on film, are considered one of the greatest clubs ever...with little help from Hector Lopez.

"I didn't have too good a year. I hit .222 with three home runs, something like that. I wasn't playing much. Everyone was hitting home runs. That's one of the worst years I ever had playing baseball."

But in Game Five of the World Series, Lopez drove in five runs in the Yankees' clinching 13-5 victory.

"That made the year for me. I did what I was supposed to."

'Whatta Pair of Hands'

This is what Hector Lopez came to be known as, not a term of endearment.

"I made three errors at third base for Casey one day. Everywhere I went, the ball followed me. The most important thing is, I made the last out of the game. I had the ball hit to me, played it off my chest and threw the guy out at first base."

That was when Dick Young hung the nickname on him.

"'What a pair of hands.' That was my boy, the sportswriter, Dick Young. But he wrote some good stuff about me, though. It didn't move me one way or another. Nineteen fifty-nine was the worst year I ever had fielding. I was a pretty good fielder. That was my forte, fielding the ball, making the plays. That year I didn't do too good and he gave me the business."

SPARKY LYLE

A Regular Laugh Riot

One of Sparky Lyle's favorite things to do was sitting on birthday cakes—while naked. He would be seen getting out of a coffin for laughs or give trainers and management a scare by showing up at spring training wearing fake casts.

Don't Try This At Home

Sparky Lyle posted a 13-5 record and 26 saves in helping the Yankees win the 1977 World Series championship.

Always the flake, Lyle took his championship ring and tried to cut the glass on his coffee table at home.

"Then I found out that the coffee table was worth more than my ring," he quipped.

*　*　*　*

Sparky Lyle proved to be the Yankees' top relief specialist during the 1970s.

As effective as he was on the field, his off-field antics raised eyebrows. Lyle had a penchant for sitting naked on birthday cakes. He also had his teammates rolling in laughter after a life-after-death stunt one day.

Fred Stanley had a friend deliver a casket to the clubhouse, a way station before he converted it into a bar for his van. Lyle couldn't resist the opportunity to spring forth from the coffin, so he got dressed up in a hood-like surgical mask and painted the area around his eyes black.

Manager Bill Virdon liked to conduct pregame meetings and go over the opponent's strengths and weaknesses. Prior to the meeting, Lyle climbed into the casket and waited for the right moment to arise.

As Virdon went through a description of the Baltimore Orioles lineup, Lyle pushed open the top, sat up and said, "How dooooo yoooooou pitch to Brooks Ro-been-son?"

Virdon couldn't help but laugh, although he threatened to have Lyle remain in the coffin.

✻   ✻   ✻   ✻

A pitcher's arm is his lifeblood, and Sparky Lyle wasn't going to have just any medical expert examine his wing.

Lyle's trainer with minor league club Winston-Salem (North Carolina) was a fellow named John Dennai. He was examining the arm of pitcher Kenny Wright one night and said, "Yep, looks like a case of tenderitis."

A perplexed Wright answered, "You mean tendinitis, don't you?" Dennai said, "Well, it's either tenderitis or tendinitis, one of those two."

Needless to say, Lyle refused to have Dennai check out his arm.

✻   ✻   ✻   ✻

Sparky Lyle earned the American League Cy Young Award following a 1977 season during which he posted a 13-5 record and 2.17 earned run average over 72 appearances. His 26 saves certainly caught the attention of the Cy Young voters.

When a reporter asked Lyle what he was going to do with the award, Lyle told him he was going to build a lighted trophy case on his lawn and leave the plaque out there for 10 years.

"He wasn't sure whether to believe me or not," Lyle said later.

✱   ✱   ✱   ✱

Sparky Lyle made his major league debut with the Boston Red Sox.

In one of his early outings in Kansas City, Lyle was paired up with ex-Yankees catcher Elston Howard. Twice he shook off Howard's pitch call only to throw two balls and eventually walk the batter. Manager Dick Williams, as tough as they come, immediately gave Lyle the hook.

Afterwards, veteran Carl Yastrzemski questioned how a rookie could shake off a veteran catcher like that. Williams agreed and threatened to fine Lyle the next time he did that.

Howard then showed why he was such a pitcher's friend. He thought Williams' decision was wrong, and so he devised a system with Lyle whereby if the pitcher wanted to shake off a pitch call all he had to do was delay his windup for a bit more time. With the acknowledgment, Howard would then flash new signals.

✱   ✱   ✱   ✱

Sparky Lyle was rewarded with a contract extension and raise following his being named American League Cy Young Award winner in 1977.

However, that winter owner George Steinbrenner opened his checkbook for some incoming pitchers, some of whom commanded more salary than the veteran Lyle. The reliever was upset and held out at the start of 1978's spring training.

Following several frantic phone calls from Yankees' front office personnel, Lyle finally agreed to report some four days late. When Lyle and his wife arrived at the airport in Fort Lauderdale, Florida, Steinbrenner adviser Cedric Tallis greeted the Lyles, as did a 100-piece high school band which played "Pomp and Circumstance," the tune that usually greeted Lyle on his trips out of the Yankee Stadium bullpen.

MICKEY MANTLE

Worth Something

An autograph or a home run ball from Mickey Mantle was a prize to keep, even before he reached the major leagues.

Playing for the Joplin (Missouri) Miners, a Class C team in the Western Association, a powerful Mantle would often hit home runs that would clear the right field fence and sometimes carry into an orphanage.

One time, after he drove a home run through a window, the children hung out a sign saying: "THANKS FOR THE BALL, MICKEY!"

In fact, somewhere lies a trophy case signed by Mantle.

When the 1962 All-Star Game wrapped up, Mantle shared a taxi with American League All-Stars Rich Rollins and Camilo Pascual.

While the cab was stopped, a fan called out to Mantle asking to sign his trophy case. Mantle stepped out of the cab, crossed the street and did just that.

Wait, There's More

Fans who watched Mickey Mantle in his later playing days realized the rigors of everyday baseball life, a lack of proper

Mickey Mantle

training and well-publicized social outings took a toll on his body.

When Mantle was breaking into the pros, the first thing that caught scouts' attentions was his tremendous bat power. The second thing was his speed—soon enough the scribes were calling Mantle "The Commerce Comet," named after his hometown in Oklahoma. A New York sports writer timed Mantle from home plate to first base in 3.1 seconds, when no other athlete had been clocked in less than 3.4 seconds.

Bill Dickey told some writers, "You should time him on his way to second, when he's really moving. Nobody who ever lived can reach second base from the plate as quickly as Mickey Mantle."

With All His Might

Mantle had one approach at the plate: swing the bat hard.

He never bought into the scholarly approach used by Boston Red Sox great Ted Williams. In fact, when the Splendid Splinter shared some of his tips with the Mick, Mantle's head would spin.

The mighty swing produced some prodigious blasts. On April 17, 1953, at Griffith Stadium in Washington, D.C., Mantle hit a ball off Senators pitcher Chuck Stobbs that carried out of the ballpark. It first cleared a 55-foot high wall behind the left field bleachers, bounced off a 60-foot sign and came to rest in the backyard of a nearby house.

A Yankees public relations man announced the shot as traveling 565 feet, although years later he admitted to have never left the ballpark to measure. The bat and ball were later sent to the National Baseball Hall of Fame at Cooperstown, New York.

For Your Information . . .

Sometimes it wasn't pure might which led to Mantle's success at the plate.

Bob Turley, who pitched for the Yankees from 1955-62, often studied the tendencies of opposing hurlers, and relayed useful information to Mantle.

Said Turley: "One day on the bench I was sitting next to Mantle and showed him that I could predict all the pitches. He said, 'God almighty, let's work something out.' So during all my years in New York, Mickey and I would have all kinds of signs based on my whistling to let him know what was coming."

Loosey-goosey?

Mickey Mantle had an uneven temperament, running from hot to cold on a daily basis. Of course, he had his loose side, and he wasn't afraid to show it to his teammates in a tight spot.

The Milwaukee Braves took a three-games-to-one lead in the 1958 World Series. Mantle showed up in the locker room wearing a trick arrow on his head, as if someone had shot him through the head.

He told his teammates they were in a tough bind and broke up the locker room with a cross-eyed face.

The Yankees came back to win that series in seven games.

No Fish Story

Mantle wasn't afraid to scam his teammates when a humorous opportunity arose.

One time he solicited dollars for a raffle of a ham, only there was no ham. Purloined of his pork prize, Jim Bouton got even during Mantle's fishing derby, winning the weight division title with a 10-pound fish he had bought in the store a day earlier.

Livin' (Not So) Large

The first professional contract Mickey Mantle signed in 1949 was for $400 to finish out a minor league season.

For his rookie season of 1951, the Yankees paid him $7,500.

The following year was the same, although he would receive a $2,500 bonus for staying on the roster until June.

Mickey and his wife, Merlyn, rented a small room at the Concourse Plaza Hotel. It had no stove, no refrigerator and no television set.

"We couldn't afford to rent a television set, at $10 a month," Merlyn said. "Mickey needed to send money home to help his family."

In retirement, Mantle made so much more.

With baseball card and collectible shows becoming ever so popular in the 1980s and 1990s, all ballplayers—retired and still active—started to command large appearance fees. A three-day show could net Mantle nearly $50,000.

Hey, Mister?

In an interview with *USA Today*, Mantle told this joke: "You know, I dreamed I died, and when I got up to heaven St. Peter met me at the pearly gates and said I couldn't get in because I hadn't always been good. 'But before you go,' St. Peter said, 'God has six dozen baseballs He'd like you to sign.'

Etched In Stone

The dearly departed Mantle once told Yankee teammate Tony Kubek he wanted one thing written on his tombstone: "I was a good teammate."

ROGER MARIS

Ouch!

Roger Maris was not only a target of fans who disapproved of his chase of Babe Ruth's home run record, he also drew the ire of teammates on occasion.

Since Maris often liked to shut fans up with lines about how much money he was making ($70,000 a year), some of his teammates would encourage Maris to "hit them with your wallet."

Auspicious Beginning

It didn't take long for Roger Maris to become a Yankee legend.

His 1960 debut in pinstripes featured a single, double and two home runs.

He would finish the season with 39 home runs, one fewer than American League champion Mickey Mantle.

No Classic For Him

The World Series was not kind to Roger Maris. He batted. 187 in 28 Fall Classic games from 1960-64—but he did provide several memorable moments:

Roger Maris

• Maris homered in his first postseason at-bat.

• A year later his ninth-inning home run lifted the Yankees over the Cincinnati Reds in Game Three.

• In 1962, his fine defensive skills were displayed as he hustled to field a Willie Mays double and kept Matty Alou from scoring to secure a 1-0 triumph over the San Francisco Giants.

Pass The Mouthwash

Outlasting Mickey Mantle in the 1961 home run race and eclipsing Babe Ruth's immortal record of 60 by just one left a bitter taste with many Yankees fans who couldn't appreciate what Roger Maris had accomplished.

"People were reluctant to give me any credit," he said years later. "I thought hitting 61 home runs was something. But everyone shied off. Why, I don't know. Maybe I wasn't the chosen one, but I was the one who got the record. It would have been a helluva lot more fun if I never hit those home runs. All it brought me was headaches."

Called a "flop" by some writers after hitting 33 home runs the following season, Maris grew increasingly disenchanted as fans derided his home run production which dropped to 23, 26, eight and 13 the next four seasons. He was subsequently traded to the St. Louis Cardinals, a club he helped to win National League pennants in 1967 and 1968.

Forgiven

Maris stayed away from a number of Old-Timer's Games, but he did return to the 1978 affair at Yankee Stadium. He was surprised when he received warm cheers.

"It's like obituaries. When you die, they give you good reviews," he said.

Welcome, Rog!

Roger Maris came from humble roots, so playing in New York was quite a shock for him.

"This city's too big," Maris was quoted as saying.

At least roommate Bob Cerv didn't believe him. "Don't ever let anybody tell you they don't like coming to a team like the Yankees," Cerv said. "The Yankees are over the tracks and up the hill."

At least Maris would have appreciated a nicer reception when he arrived in the winter of 1959 in a trade with Kansas City. Problem is, he was dealt for popular Yankee Hank Bauer.

"For the first few games I used to hear guys yelling for Bauer," Maris said, who silenced any naysayers with 39 home runs and 112 runs batted in during his 1960 season. A year later, he would break Babe Ruth's home run record with 61.

BILLY MARTIN

The Glasses Come Off

Billy Martin was born Alfred Manuel (Billy) Pesano, but many people who crossed his path got to know him as Battling Billy.

One time Boston Red Sox rookie Jimmy Piersall tossed insults at Martin about his big nose, so Martin threw some rights and lefts at him under the grandstand at Fenway Park to settle the score.

Sometimes Martin used a little help. One day St. Louis Browns catcher Clint Courtney spiked shortstop Phil Rizzuto while sliding into second base. Martin started a brawl with Courtney, eventually knocking his glasses off. That's when Whitey Ford literally stepped in and smashed the glasses.

Yer Outta Here!

Martin was run out of plenty of ballgames by umpires, but perhaps none as bizarre as one night in Arlington, Texas.

A handful of calls had already gone against the Yankees and Martin had exercised his right to argue on several occasions.

Martin stewed in the dugout and shifted the cap on his head so the bill faced sideways. The umpire motioned for

Billy Martin

Martin to come out of the dugout and ordered the manager to fix his cap.

Martin refused and was promptly ejected, but not before kicking dirt on the shoes of the offended arbiter.

On Billy Martin:

"He's the kind of guy you'd like to kill if he's playing on the other team, but you'd like 10 of him on your side."
— Cleveland Indians general manager Frank Lane.

The Ol' Pine Tar Game

No one will ever accuse of Yankees manager Billy Martin of not taking advantage of any edge one of his players had or a verse in a rules book.

That approach brought about one of the strangest game circumstances of all time.

On July 24, 1983, the Yankees carried a 4-3 lead into the last inning of a game with the Kansas City Royals. That all changed when Brett deposited a two-out Goose Gossage offering into the right-field seats to give the Royals a 5-4 lead.

Martin went out to Tim McClelland and asked the home plate umpire to check the amount of pine tar on Brett's bat. Resting the bat across the 17-inch plate, McClelland noticed clearly the pine tar extended past the 18 inches allowable as set forth in the rules book. The home run would be disallowed.

So McClelland turned to the third base dugout, threw his thumb in the air to signal an out that ended the game. Brett was enraged, storming the field to confront McClelland. Brett had to be restrained by members of the Royals.

Meanwhile, the bat in question disappeared. Kansas City pitcher Gaylord Perry got a hold of it in the dugout and passed it to Steve Renko, who in turn handed it to Hal McRae. Eventually, the umpires had to retrieve the bat from the Royals clubhouse.

Third baseman Graig Nettles ribbed his buddy Gossage afterward.

"You came in and gave up a home and got a save?" Nettles asked.

"I'll take them any way I can get them," Goose replied.

The Yankees thought they had gotten away with a sneaky win. However, American League president Lee MacPhail overturned the decision, stating McClelland's ruling wasn't in line with "the spirit of the rule." He ordered the game to be picked up at a later date, with Brett's home run standing and the next batter up.

The Yankees resisted and almost didn't show up for the second finish, an affair which took 10 minutes on an off day set for August 18. The final four batters of the game—one for Kansas City and three for the Yankees—were retired.

"Mentally it really hurt us," Martin said. "We felt we had a game taken away from us because of a play that was illegal. It was hard for our guys to accept."

*   *   *   *

It was Mickey Mantle who introduced Billy Martin to the pleasures of hunting when they were Yankee teammates. Often they would go out hunting for ducks and other waterfowl.

On one offseason trip to Texas, Mantle played one of his legendary practical jokes on an unsuspecting Martin, only the plan backfired, so to speak.

Mantle had Martin stay in the car while he went into the house of a friend who was going to allow them to hunt deer on his property. While inside, Mantle's friend asked if Mickey would be willing to put down his ailing mule as a favor. Mantle agreed, but he didn't let on to Martin.

Mantle stormed out of the house and told Martin his friend wouldn't allow them to hunt on his property. "You got to be kidding," Martin said, shocked at the news following a five-hour drive. Mantle said, "No, I'm not, and I'm so mad that I'm going to go by the barn and shoot his mule."

Martin insisted Mantle not do it, but Mantle drove his car over to the barnyard, spotted the mule and let off a rifle shot into the sight-impaired critter.

Next thing Mantle knew, Martin let loose two rifle shots. "What the hell are you doing?" Mantle demanded. Martin had shot two of the farmer's cows, for which the ballplayers had to ante up some money.

*   *   *   *

Sometimes there are no cures to a losing streak. On several occasions during his managerial career, Billy Martin would throw the names of the nine players he wanted in the lineup into a hat and would have someone pull the names out to draw up the batting lineup.

*   *   *   *

Billy Martin brawled with opponents as much as he tangled with Yankee team members. However, his infamous Billy The Kid nickname was not conjured up from the famed gunslinger.

Casey Stengel was managing the 1948 Oakland Oaks of the Pacific Coast League. His club was made up of many veteran major leaguers who were let go or were longtime members of the P.C.L. Since Martin was the youngest member of the lineup known as the Nine Old Men, the nickname Billy The Kid seemed appropriate.

DON MATTINGLY

Listen to Mike Easler talk about his time with Don Mattingly. "He epitomized that passion and desire for the game. I was there in '87 when he had seven consecutive games with home runs. I'm telling you, Donnie Mattingly was my hero. As a matter of fact, I came over with the nickname 'The Hit Man' and when I left his nickname was 'The Hit Man.' He took it. Shame on him. But that's New York for you."

Showdown

One of the highlights of Ron Kittle's stay with the Yankees was watching Don Mattingly and Wade Boggs wage a battle for the batting title on the final day of the season in Boston.

"Donnie had to go 5-for-5. I think he went 4-for-5 and his last at-bat was a line drive to shortstop that Eddie Romero caught. Wade Boggs sat out the game and he's on the big screen smiling and nodding his head. All of a sudden, you see him putting on his batting gloves because if Donnie gets a hit, he would have had to bat the next inning to win the title. Just seeing all that stuff going on was pretty remarkable."

There's a story inside that story.

"I'm hitting behind Donnie that day and he broke a bat. I grabbed the bat and I just yelled up to the stands, '100 bucks for a Mattingly bat.' Sure enough, some guy whips out a $100 bill. Lou Piniella is managing and he says, "Only Ronnie Kittle could do that.""

Donnie Baseball?

If Boston Celtics great Larry Bird is called "The Hick from French Lick," then fellow Hoosier resident Don Mattingly could accept being called naive upon his signing with the Yankees in 1979.

"Honestly, at one time I thought Babe Ruth was a cartoon character," said Mattingly, blaming his Indiana background on his failed baseball history lesson.

Um, Wrong Call

Early in the 1985 season, Don Mattingly told the media he thought a day off was more important than attending an optional workout during the midst of a tough stretch of games.

George Steinbrenner jumped all over Mattingly's comments.

"I'm disappointed in that young man's attitude," he said, citing the failure to show up as a lack of discipline.

Ten years later, Mattingly was roundly praised as the best Yankee player not to have played in a World Series. The left-handed hitting first baseman was not only named the 10th captain in team history but also finished a stellar 14-year career with a .307 average, 222 home runs and 1,099 runs batted in.

Don Mattingly

Work, Work, Work

Putting in time to work on his game was never a problem for Don Mattingly.

While attending Reitz Memorial High School in Evansville, Indiana, Mattingly used to take two hours of batting practice even before the team's regularly scheduled three-hour practices. It's no wonder Mattingly batted over .500 in both his junior and senior years, and led Reitz to an Indiana state title.

It was the same high school that a four-year-old Mattingly served as mascot.

Cap'n Don

Don Mattingly joined a distinguished list of Yankee captains in 1991. He led by example and by work ethic.

A mild-mannered Midwesterner, Mattingly knew when to pick his spots to address teammates.

In the midst of a minor hitting slump, Paul O'Neill had asked a coach if he would ever get another hit. Mattingly chimed in, "No, with that tired swing you may not."

A simple kick in the butt, from one perfectionist to another.

Movin' On Up

The year Don Mattingly claimed the American League batting title (1984), he wasn't even the starting first baseman at the outset.

Ken Griffey Sr. had that job. It didn't take long for manager Yogi Berra to make a switch, though.

Mattingly finished up edging teammate Dave Winfield for the batting crown (.343). He collected 207 hits, 110 runs batted in, 44 doubles and 23 home runs. He also led the AL in fielding with only five errors to his credit.

No Ring-a-ding-ding(s)

Don Mattingly batted .307 in 14 seasons as a New York Yankee. Unfortunately for him, he made the ballclub one year after a World Series appearance and left one year before its next, thus giving him the distinction—if you can call it that—of being the best Yankee ever to miss the Fall Classic.

Perhaps that is why Yankee fans—sensing the possible end to a great career—erupted when Mattingly saw his first playoff action in the 1995 American League Divisional Series with the Seattle Mariners.

The applause brought tears to the eyes of manager Buck Showalter, a former minor league teammate of Mattingly.

After hitting .417 in the five-game loss to the Mariners, Mattingly took the 1996 season off, barely keeping alive the notion of returning.

The Yankees beat the Atlanta Braves in the World Series, with Mattingly and his wife, Kim, watching from their home in Evansville, Indiana.

Then in January 1997, he called it quits for good.

"I am what I am, and I did what I did," Mattingly told a press gathering. "I don't feel cheated. I chose not to play."

His message to Yankee fans on Don Mattingly Day, on the last day of August 1997, matched his play.

"I tried to keep it pure," he said. "I tried to keep it simple, just play great baseball over the years. I hope you appreciated it."

The Buck Speaks Here

"People ask me all the time about whether Don Mattingly should be in the Hall of Fame," former Yankees manager Buck Showalter said. "Statistically, he might not match up, depending on what your criteria are. But he's a guy who supersedes any statistics when you evaluate him. Nobody in the history of baseball has more of a Hall-of-Fame character than Don Mattingly."

In The Blood

The athletic genes in the Mattingly family were not left for just Don. His brother Randy—almost 10 years his senior—played quarterback in the Canadian Football League.

Don On Mike

Michael Jordan gave up his basketball career to try his hand at baseball, but the Chicago Bulls star never left the minors.

Said Mattingly of the NBA scoring superstar: "I like to think, OK, Michael, you're number 23 all over the world, just not in this stadium."

JOE MCCARTHY

A Real Winner

There was only one way with longtime manager Joe McCarthy—winning. Over 21 seasons McCarthy's Yankee teams compiled 1,460 wins and a winning percentage of .627, both franchise records. His Yankee clubs won eight American League pennants and seven World Series championships.

How important was baseball and winning to McCarthy?

One day a depressed McCarthy was greeted by his wife, who tried to cheer him.

"At least we still have each other," she said. To which he replied: "Yes, dear, I know. But in the ninth inning today I would've traded you in for a sacrifice fly."

"Einstein in Flannels"

It was said Joe McCarthy read nothing during the season unless it involved baseball.

"So I eat, drink and sleep baseball 24 hours a day What's wrong with that?" he asked.

And he wanted his players thinking of nothing but baseball as well. To make his point, he had the card tables in the locker room smashed.

"This is a clubhouse, and not a club room," he said. "I want players here to think of baseball and nothing else."

Yankees general manager Ed Barrow said McCarthy's memory was one of the best he came across, a good thing considering McCarthy never took notes and never used charts. Pitcher Lefty Gomez tabbed McCarthy "Einstein in flannels."

Speaking of flannels, McCarthy actually had the team's caps and uniforms cut larger so his players would look bigger and stronger.

The Right Way

Joe McCarthy was a stickler for Yankee image long before George Steinbrenner happened along.

Jackets and ties were the order for road trips. So, too, were the team breakfast sessions set for 8:30 a.m.

In 1936, McCarthy drew up a famous list which became his Ten Commandments of Baseball.

1. Nobody ever became a ballplayer by walking after a ball.
2. You will never become a .300 hitter unless you take that bat off your shoulder.
3. An outfielder who throws back of the runner is locking the barn door after the horse is stolen.
4. Keep your head up, and you may not have to keep it down.
5. When you start to slide, S-L-I-D-E. He who changes his mind may have to change a good leg for a bad one.
6. Do not alibi on bad hops. Anybody can field a good one.
7. Always run them out. You can never tell.
8. Do not quit.

9. Do not find too much fault with the umpires. You cannot expect them to be as perfect as you are.
10. A pitcher who hasn't control hasn't anything.

Harumph!

Several sports writers took to calling Joe McCarthy the "push-button manager," once his team started winning, as if the players would win without their helmsman.

"I spend all my summers in Atlantic City and only come back for the World Series," McCarthy would grumble aloud.

The Point Is...

Joe McCarthy picked a weird stage to prove a point. As manager of the American League All-Star Team in 1943, McCarthy did not use any of the six Yankees picked for the game to prove that he could beat the National League All-Stars without them.

He was right. The A.L. prevailed, 8-5.

GIL MCDOUGALD

I Can Hear Clearly Now

Just the very act of calling Gil McDougald, the 1951 American League Rookie of the Year, for a phone interview for this book could be filed under the term 'miracle.'

McDougald had gradually gone deaf in both ears after a freak accident in which he was hit above the right ear by a line drive during batting practice in 1955.

A cochlear implant behind his right ear changed everything.

"It's funny. When you've been deaf for 15 years and then all of a sudden, things change."

Turns out a newspaper column in the *New York Times* that described McDougald's plight was read by a doctor in Washington D.C..

"He picked it up and he happened to be a Yankee fan. He called my wife right away. I don't even think it was 9 o'clock in the morning and he already had set up the appointment. What happens is you find out when you're entirely deaf that it is a hearing world. And if you can't communicate, it is really difficult."

Gil McDougald can now hear the joy and squeals of delight from his 11 grandchildren.

Something That May Never Happen Again

It's one thing to switch positions twice. It's quite something else to play all three positions, second, short and third, with such distinction as to make the All-Star team at each spot.

But that's exactly what Gil McDougald accomplished in the 50s, something no one has done since.

"I think anybody can play the three positions. But there's no way you can play three positions constantly and do the job you'd like to do. If you stayed at one position, you gotta be better because you get more used to the position and don't have to make adjustments every day."

SAM MCDOWELL

Pitching on Fumes

In 1973, the Yankees acquired Sam McDowell from San Francisco, who had traded away future Hall of Famer Gaylord Perry, to get him. "Being an alcoholic, I met the team in Oakland and showed up drunk from the night before. Fortunately, I sobered up. I did fairly well for a while because I was kind of a semi-controlled drunk. When I say 'semi-controlled', most of most career I was a control drunk in which I never drank the night before or the day that I was pitching thinking somehow that would help me. Most of it was superstition and had nothing to do with drinking because, of course, I never knew I had a problem. The denial was so strong in me as it is in, I guess, everybody.

"Then my arm in the middle of the season started to hurt. That was when my drinking just kept escalating."

Helping Others to Help Themselves

Recovery. That is the theme of Sam McDowell's post-baseball-playing life, his and others. "What was sad was after I was thrown out of baseball by the Pittsburgh Pirates and eventually went through my own recovery, I still didn't believe that I had the right to help anybody else. I was just so frightened and scared of hurting somebody by giving them any advice. I just kind of stayed to myself."

Eventually, McDowell went to Pitt for course work to understand the intricacies of drug and alcohol addiction and to understand different types of therapies.

"I became a therapist and figured that since I burned too many bridges in baseball and would never be asked back, I went ahead and started my own practice with teenagers trying to help them with their difficulties and problems."

For 18 years, Sam McDowell was the therapist for the Texas Rangers in sports psychology, addictions and prevention programs. He has also been a consulting therapist for the Baseball Assistance Team for the past 14 years.

BILL MONBOQUETTE

Don't Shut the Door

Bill Monboquette was the only reliable starter for a series of horrible Boston clubs throughout the early 60s. The rotation was Bill Monboquette and then wait four days. After being dealt to Detroit, he was released and then signed with the Yankees in 1967.

"We had a rookie on our club by the name of Charlie Sands. Mantle, I guess, got talking with Ralph Houk, and said, 'We'll set him up.'"

There was one rule about paying a visit to The Major's office.

"If you had to go in, you don't shut the door. Mantle went over to Charlie and said, 'Ralph wants to see you.' And of course, Charlie didn't know what to think. 'What does he want to see me for?'"

Mantle told Sands, "When you go in there, make sure you don't shut the door." Apparently, once upon a time, somebody did shut the door and Houk got ticked at him. A reputation was born.

"So Charlie went in and Ralph said, 'Shut the door.' And Sands said, 'No way, I'm not shutting the door.' Again, Ralph says, 'Shut the door.' And Sands says, 'I can't shut the door.' Ralph then threatened him, 'If you don't shut the door....'"

"I guess it was so funny that Ralph couldn't hold it back and he started to laugh. Mantle was going absolutely bananas. He loved to do things like that. I was dying laughing myself."

Playing With the Hall of Fame

Bill Monboquette's career spanned a living, breathing Hall of Fame.

"I had the privilege of playing three years with Ted Williams, five with Yastrzemski, a little more than a year and a half with Kaline in Detroit, and then I played with Mantle and Ford. Then I got traded to San Francisco for Lindy McDaniel and I got a chance to play with Mays, McCovey, Marichal and Perry."

All of which fell on deaf ears one day.

"I told the kids this one time when I was coaching for the Bluejays in St. Catherine's. A couple of guys said to me, 'Well, who are they?' and now I was really mad then. I said, 'Well, I'll tell you what. They're all Hall of Famers and they never acted like you kids do.' I think they got the message right there. The respect for the game, I don't know if it's there like it used to be. It's a shame because it's an awful great game."

WILCY MOORE

Getting Even (Sort Off)

A most improbable Yankee was an Oklahoman named Wilcy Moore. General manager Ed Barrow had read an article in 1926 about a strong right-hander who had run up a 20-1 record in the Piedmont League. Despite protestations from a scouting staff that felt a 30-year-old hurler was too old, Barrow signed him sight unseen.

"Anyone who has a 20-1 record anywhere is worth taking a look at," Barrow said.

His instincts were correct. Wilcy went on to post a 19-7 record (6-6 as a starter) with 13 saves and a 2.28 earned run average in 1927. He went on to win a World Series game in both 1927 and 1928.

Moore went 29-15 from 1927-29 and, after two years away, went 7-6 in 1932-33.

As good as Moore was on the mound, he was awful at the plate. He batted .080 in 1927 (.102 in his career).

No doubt, he became a favorite of Babe Ruth, who used to tease Moore about his hitting. Ruth even bet Moore he wouldn't get more than three hits in a season. Moore won the bet, with six hits in 75 at-bats. He used the $300 to buy two mules for his farm, naming one Babe and the other Ruth.

ROSS MOSCHITTO

Mickey's Caddie

They are a small group of players, players who spelled The Mick in centerfield in the late innings in spacious Yankee Stadium. The last is remembered best, Ross Moschitto, number 53.

Despite what major league records say, he could hit. He hit so well at Johnson City in the Appalachian Rookie League in 1964 that he was named the Player of the Year.

In 1965, he made the spectacular leap from Class-A to the Bronx, just in time to be part of the beginning of the end after five straight appearances in the World Series.

"I felt almost like I was a jinx. That's one reason why I signed with the New York Yankees. I had other offers from St. Louis and the Mets. The Yankees were a championship team. I get there and they're at the bottom of the heap."

In a 110-game career, he batted just 36 times. One of those was a home run.

"It was one of those real laughers. We were losing something like 15-2. We had just come off a roadtrip from LA where I actually went 2-for-2. So that game I got in early. Mickey had hit a home run earlier."

Moschitto was facing Jim Perry, Gaylord's older brother.

"He threw me a slider inside and I swung at it and missed. Then he got one up and in and I creamed it to leftfield."

The papers jumped on the story.

"They were saying 'The Next DiMaggio' and that I was hitting them where Joe D hit them and all this nonsense."

His parents still have the ball at their home in California.

THURMAN MUNSON

(Not) Your Man For The Job

Manager Billy Martin named Thurman Munson captain of the New York Yankees in 1976, the team's first one since 1939 when Lou Gehrig retired. While honored, Munson was also forthcoming about himself. "I'll be a terrible captain," he said. "I'm too belligerent. I cuss and swear at people. I yell at umpires, and maybe I'm a little too tough at home. I don't sign autographs like I should and I haven't always been very good with the writers."

Kiss And Run (Home)

Thurman Munson was a three-sport star in high school.

To help stay in shape, Thurman would include seeing his girlfriend in his training plans.

"He was always playing some kind of sport," said Diane Munson, who knew Thurman since he was 10 years old and later married him.

"To stay in shape he would run the mile to my house, kiss me and run right back home."

Thurman Munson

.300? Absolutely!

There was no settling for mediocrity with young Thurman Munson. Once told by manager, Ralph Houk, that he, a rookie, shouldn't be too concerned about hitting around .240 since .250 is all the club expected, Munson shot back: "Damnit. I can hit .300 in this league."

True to his word, Munson batted .302 and became the first catcher to win the American League Rookie of the Year award in 1970.

Move Over, Shamu?

Standing 5-foot-11 and weighing 190 pounds, Thurman Munson resembled a football player more than a baseball man.

Busing to a spring training game in Florida one day, teammate Lou Piniella called out to the driver. "Hey, Bussy, let the walrus off at Sea World."

At least Piniella got a smile out of Munson.

"My build works against me," Munson said. "I'm a short, chunky guy. I'm not the athletic hero type. Fisk is tall, lean and more attractive."

Fisk was none other than Boston Red Sox backstop Carlton Fisk.

There was a fierce rivalry between the two throughout the 1970s as they were the top catchers the American League could offer.

"He got all the publicity and most of the All-Star votes," Munson recalled, "I don't hold it against him personally, but he's never been as good a catcher as I am. If we were on the same team, I might even like him, but he'd have to play another position."

Expert Foresight

Financial security was foremost in Thurman Munson's mind as his career headed toward the end, but came earlier in a fatal plane crash.

Apparently, Munson was a sound businessman whose real estate and other ventures netted his family more $1 million.

Munson's financial dealings allowed him a few extravagances. That is why Munson learned to fly and bought a small jet plane. He figured the plane would afford him the chance to fly home to Ohio on occasion to spend time with his family.

However, Munson advanced to small jets too quickly, said his teammates.

On August 2, 1979, Munson was in the pilot's seat when the jet he was trying to land at Akron-Canton Airport crashed. Munson broke his neck and never got out of the plane, which went up in flames.

A Best Friend's Feat

Thurman Munson was one of Bobby Murcer's closest friends on the Yankees. Murcer had been reacquired from the Chicago Cubs only weeks before Munson's untimely death.

Murcer delivered a heartfelt eulogy at Munson's funeral in Ohio and, later that evening, honored his friend and team captain the best way he knew how.

The Yankees flew home from Ohio that very same afternoon. A somber crowd at Yankee Stadium watched the Baltimore Orioles jump out to a 4-0 lead. The Yankees drew closer as Murcer hit a three-run home run, his first Stadium home run in six years.

In the bottom of the ninth inning, Bucky Dent walked and Willie Randolph's sacrifice bunt attempt was botched by pitcher

Tippy Martinez. Up stepped Murcer. Down 0-2 in the count, Murcer drove both runners in with a single to left.

The Yankee dugout emptied and mobbed Murcer at the bag.

"Everybody was so tired," Murcer said. "I think we were playing in the spirit of Thurman. I think that's what carried us through the game."

∗   ∗   ∗   ∗

The clean-cut image that the Yankees adhered to for many years also allowed for simple protests.

Catcher Thurman Munson was upset with the way owner George Steinbrenner was handling Billy Martin's job status, so he grew a beard in protest. It turned out to be a huge furor in New York as the daily newspapers played it up with hair-raising appeal.

As a favor to Martin, Munson eventually shaved the beard in order to take the pressure off the embattled manager.

BOBBY MURCER

Over the Mountain and Through the Woods

C arl Yastrzemski stepped to the plate one afternoon in the old Stadium with 399 career home runs and an inviting short porch in right for his lethal lefthanded stroke. Bobby Murcer was playing center, Ron Woods, acquired for Tom Tresh, was in right.

Murcer picks up the story.

"Yaz hits a line drive to right and the last you see of Woods, he is leaping up and you could see the ball in the glove and he disappears in the stands. There's nobody over there. I'm the only one that got there quick enough. He's knocked out colder than a cucumber."

The glove and the ball are nearby. That's when Murcer went to work.

"I kind of put the glove up towards his hand and put the ball in the glove. The umpire, of course, is running out there, and when he got there, he looked in the stands. He saw the ball in the glove and called him out. They had a pretty big argument. Yaz came all the way out to rightfield to argue that play. If it wasn't for me, he probably would have been there a lot sooner with his 3,000th hit for sure."

Playing the Monuments

Long before there was videotape, there was film. And there is film of Bobby Murcer playing center field in cavernous Yankee Stadium chasing balls bouncing in, around and through the monuments, which stood on the field of play. This was not unlike less accomplished ballplayers chasing Spaldeens underneath parked cars during stickball games in the Bronx as runners circled the bases.

"Not too many balls ever got out to that area. If they did, they were either bouncing or rolling. Not too many were hit in the air. Even though the monuments were on the field, they really didn't come into play as far as them being obstructive to you trying to catch a fly ball.

"It was like 463 feet and that was during the dead-ball era anyway. I chased balls in and around and in the back side of the monuments several times. A couple of times, I actually slid through them to try to cut a ball off that went in one side."

The Prodigal Son Returns

August 6, 1979, the day Thurman Munson was buried in Ohio, was one of the highlights in the career for Bobby Murcer, one of his best friends on the club.

"Billy Martin wasn't going to play me. He said, 'Take the night off. You're tired, you haven't had any sleep in two nights.' I said, 'I feel like I need to play.' And he said, 'Do you want to?' And I said, 'Yes, I really do want to play.' The unusual thing was Billy left me in there late in the game. At that time, they were pinch-hitting me and Lou. He left me in there against Tippy Martinez with the game on the line and that's when I got another base hit, a double down the leftfield line. Who knows why Billy did that?"

Murcer also struck a three-run homer and finished with five RBIs as the Yankees came back from a 5-0 deficit to win 6-5 in yet another unforgettable night inside Yankee Stadium.

JERRY NARRON

A Night Like None Other

Thurman Munson died in a plane crash on a Thursday, August 2, 1979, an off-day for the Yankees. The Baltimore Orioles arrived for a weekend series that night. On Friday night, in one of the most emotional scenes in the Stadium's grand history, eight players took the field. It fell upon rookie Jerry Narron to do the catching. He was still in shock over the tragic death of the Yankee captain: "Ron Davis and I were living together in Dumont, New Jersey. I believe Catfish called us."

That's like one of those moments where you drop the phone.

"Absolutely."

But there were games to be played.

"I got to the Stadium Friday afternoon and everybody was just heartbroken. Before the game they told me that for the National Anthem they were gonna leave home plate vacant and that there would be a moment of silence."

Narron was told to go out on the field after that.

"I will never forget that night. I don't know if I'll ever be in a situation as difficult to play or perform or compete in a game as that was for me."

But perform he did.

"I think one thing about all professional athletes and that we're trying to focus on the competition at that moment we're playing and I think it helped me through that game. I think it helped everybody on our club through that game."

Times change but circumstances don't.

"I think that attitude has helped everybody over the last few months that are professional athletes after what happened on September 11."

Munson's passing was the death-knell for the Yankees' season. Ask Jerry Narron how he got through those ensuing days and weeks and he says, "I don't think our club did at all. I think it took until the next season for them to recover. I got traded that winter but I really believe that after Thurman got killed, we had no chance of winning the rest of the way."

Unforgettable

There are two special people in Jerry Narron's baseball life. "One is Johnny Oates and the other is Catfish Hunter. With Catfish, when I made the club in '79, I was not married and was there by myself. He let me move in with him until his family got there in June. I mean he really showed me the ropes of how it was to be a major league player."

And then there was this about Catfish.

"The first time I was gonna catch him in the big leagues we were playing the Orioles at home. I was gonna go over the club with him and he said, 'Don't worry about it, I'm gonna throw every pitch you call for. If I don't like it, I'll just throw it so they can't hit it.' That was just unbelievable, to show what kind of guy he is, working with a young catcher and taking full responsibility like that."

GRAIG NETTLES

The Other Guys

Athletes like nothing better than being appreciated with a healthy round of applause from the fans. It's the booing that drives them crazy. Graig Nettles was able to reason away the derision he sometimes encountered while playing at Yankee Stadium. "Since it's a two-team town, to keep my sanity I preferred to think that many of those who were booing me were Mets fans."

Exhibitions? Hah!

Nettles was never a fan of exhibition games. He openly derided the significance of the annual Mayor's Trophy contests between the Mets and Yankees. He also hated the exhibitions with the Yankees' upper-level farm teams.

"As a player you don't have your heart in them 100 percent because you know it doesn't count in the standings, and therefore, when you're not trying 100 percent, you don't go all out, and that's how you get hurt."

Sure enough, during an April 1983 exhibition at Nashville, second baseman Willie Randolph twisted a knee, designated

Graig Nettles

hitter Don Baylor pulled a hamstring and pitcher Dale Murray damaged his toe.

Still, Nettles—who didn't play that evening—took a bit of satisfaction in watching Nashville rally for five runs to beat the Yankees.

"Those kids were as happy as if they had won the World Series," he said. "They were giving high-fives all over the field.... Most of those kids will never make it to the big leagues, but it'll be something they can look back to their whole life."

Testing: 1, 2, 3

Some umpires are confrontational, others like to make judgments on players. Graig Nettles and arbiter Ed Runge hit it off right from the start. Runge had developed a reputation for testing rookies, and fortunately Nettles knew this. In his second major league at-bat, Runge and Nettles shared talk about their San Diego backgrounds while the pitcher and catcher were out at the mound. Runge wished him well and promptly called a pitch that Joel Horlen had nearly bounced a strike. Nettles said nothing.

The next pitch was clearly a strike and Runge issued a ball.

"He gave me pitches like no other umpire," Nettles said, "because I didn't complain to him when he tested me....Accept the calls, because in the long run you'll get the breaks."

He Got His Wish

Outspoken and moody, Graig Nettles was named the sixth captain of the New York Yankees in January 1982. This is the same third baseman who once said: "When I was a kid, I wanted to play baseball and join the circus. With the Yankees, I've been able to do both."

Outta Here

Graig Nettles had the peculiar nickname of Puff. Why? Said baseball broadcaster Joe Garagiola: "They call him Puff because he's always provoking fights and then when they start, puff, he's gone."

JOHNNY OATES

While Johnny Oates was a back-up catcher with the Yankees, Graig Nettles was diagnosed with hepatitis. "We were in Minnesota and they informed the team we were all gonna have to go down and get injected to prevent the rest of the team from getting it. We were bused to a clinic in downtown Minneapolis where we all got in line."

Cue Yogi.

"We were all going through to get our shots and Yogi asks, 'How much do these things cost?' One of the nurses says, 'Well, Mr. Berra, they're free.' He says, 'Well, in that case, give me two of them.' That was your normal Yogi take on things."

Don't Believe What You Hear

Johnny Oates holds no illusions. He knew his place on the Yankee squad. "I was one of those guys who was the 26th guy on a 25-man ballclub.

"In 1981, I was supposed to go to Columbus as a player/coach. That was the plan when I went to spring training. But with injuries to Bruce Robinson, who came up with a rotator cuff tear, I ended up making the big league club right out of spring training."

That last night of spring training, Gene Michael told Johnny Oates he had made the club.

"I'm going through the players parking lot and George came up to me, took my hand and wished me well in Columbus. He did not know that I had already been told that I had made the ballclub. I guess he was trying to get my goat a little bit. But I caught on to him real quick. It was probably the only time in my life that I've ever been half a step ahead of George Steinbrenner."

The '81 club opened at home against Texas for three games, went to Toronto for three and then to Texas, where circumstances intervened.

"I think it was a Friday night in Texas and Rick Cerone, the starting catcher, broke his thumb. I went from a player/coach in Triple-A to the starting catcher for the New York Yankees in a matter of a few days.

"I was thrilled."

Yet, Oates was brutally realistic about his state in life.

"I couldn't play anymore and they knew that before they even started me. But I had to start four or five days in a row until they picked up Barry Foote. He came in, had a great April and I was released when Cerone came off the DL.

"It was quite a story for me coming off the garbage heap to the starting catcher for the New York Yankees."

SPIKE OWEN

Spike Owen preceded his University of Texas teammate, Roger Clemens, to the home team clubhouse in the Bronx. After playing four years in Montreal, Owen became a free agent after the 1992 season. He signed a three-year contract with the Yankees and started the home opener at shortstop.

"We opened up on the road that year in Cleveland and then went to Chicago before we came home. The atmosphere in parks like Yankee Stadium is so unique and hard to beat with the history and all the great players and all the ghosts. I'm very well aware of all that stuff. Running out on the field and looking up was an amazing feeling.

"To see the Stadium jam-packed for a beautiful day game even when I talk about it now, it still gives me goosebumps to think I was out there and part of that game."

Owen was very nervous but less so once he got out there.

"I got a ground ball in the first inning which helped. I was batting ninth as usual. The big moment for me was my first time up in the second or third inning and I got a base hit in my first at bat in Yankee Stadium as a Yankee. That's a fond memory."

That gave Owen approximately 56,000 new best friends.

"I feel so fortunate in my career that I got to wear the pinstripes and play in Yankee Stadium. Unfortunately, I didn't get to spend all three of those years there and was traded to California. Being able to play in that ballpark as a Yankee is just hard to describe."

Good thing he didn't drop that first ball. As Rodney Dangerfield says, "It's a tough crowd."

East is East and West is West

Like most players, Spike Owen's career was spread out through different teams. From Seattle to Boston to Montreal to New York to California. He has always had difficulty telling friends back home in Austin, Texas that there is a profound difference in attitude.

"I got to experience a lot of teams, on the West Coast and on the East Coast and I even got to experience Montreal, another country. It is hard to put into words what East Coast baseball is like, Red Sox fans and Yankee fans. It is very intense, pressure-packed on every pitch. You can go from getting booed after one pitch or one groundball to being a hero in the very next at-bat if you do your job, whether it's a basehit or bunt or sac fly. Then they're back with you. There's a lot to that. The thing is, man, they care. They want their team to win. There's no other place like it. They actually come to that ballpark and expect you to win and you better show up to play."

That's what Owen tried to explain to people.

"We are professionals. You're getting paid to play the game. But there is a different mentality when you suit up with the pinstripes and go out and play in Yankee Stadium. I honestly believe ballplayers didn't approach things any differently when I played in Seattle or California. I know I certainly wasn't trying any less out there. But it's an intensity that's in the ballpark pretty much day in and day out. And you are aware of that."

GABE PAUL

Bad Form

Gabe Paul was a baseball executive for many years when monies were tight and he was always looking for a way to save his team a little money, even when his decisions sent the wrong message.

The Kansas City Royals and New York Yankees split the first two games of the 1977 A.L. Championship Series, and the teams traveled back to Missouri. The Royals went on to win Game Three, leaving the Yankees on the brink of elimination.

When the Yankees got back to their hotel, traveling secretary Bill Kane—under the orders of Paul—instructed the players to pack their belongings and bring their bags to the hotel lobby the next morning for check out. This would expedite matters should the Yankees lose and head back to New York right away.

George Steinbrenner found out about the request and got heaping mad. There was no way he wanted his players to think that winning Games Four and Five was out of the question, so he had Kane rescind the original requests.

The Yankees won both games, 6-4 and 5-3, to advance to the World Series, where they beat the Los Angeles Dodgers.

JOE PEPITONE

Just Put it Right There, Pal

Nobody has ever denied that Denny McLain did not groove a pitch for Mickey Mantle to hit home run #535 and surpass Jimmy Foxx. Joe Pepitone was the on-deck hitter. Here's what he saw.

"I was batting fourth, Mickey is batting third. They were beating us something like 11-3 in the ninth inning and Mantle's coming up to bat for the last time. McLain calls his catcher, Bill Freehan, out to the mound to say something to him. I think Mickey was 0-for-3 that game."

Freehan went behind the plate and Mickey stepped in.

"The next thing you know, McLain's first pitch is right down the middle. He just wound up easy and threw it. Mickey was like shocked. So Mickey looked at McLain and he pointed with his hand to throw it a little further outside."

Pepitone is on-deck watching this in disbelief.

"I'm thinking what the hell is going on here? The next pitch is right down the middle again, a nice, easy fastball that Mickey pops it up to the catcher. Freehan just stood there watching it bounce. I'm just looking at this amazed. So Mickey looks out at McLain again. He has two strikes on him. He said with his hands again to throw it a little further outside. Sure as hell, he throws it right down the middle and Mickey hits a line drive off

Joe Pepitone

the third deck that was headed for the roof at Tiger Stadium. Mickey's just running around the bases and everybody was shaking his hand."

McLain came to home plate and he's standing there with Pepitone waiting to congratulate Mantle.

"I'm asking McLain if he's still in a good mood. He's not saying anything to me. Mickey comes home and McLain shakes his hand, Freehan shakes his hand, I shake his hand and McLain goes out to the mound."

Pepitone decides he'll be the one to give McLain the signs.

"I look at McLain and I point like I want a fastball straight ahead. He shakes his head no. I give him the curve motion and he says no."

That's when Denny McLain wound up, easily threw the pitch behind him and hit Joe Pepitone right in the helmet.

"I said look at that son-of-a-bitch. That's what they do for those guys who hit all those home runs. Mickey was on the bench laughing his ass off."

And Step on it, Cabbie

Another Detroit story. "Phil Linz and I are rookies. We were just finished eating in this restaurant and we see Mantle and Ford in the lounge. They called us over."

They were impressed that these two gods wanted to talk to them.

"They tell us they're gonna go out to this place called The Flame Lounge after we eat. They say, 'Why don't you guys go there, we'll tell you where it is and we'll meet you there.' The cab ride was about $35. That was our meal money."

And that cab took them directly to The Flame Lounge, conveniently located in the heart of what was then the Detroit slums.

"It had these little round portholes on this brick building. I looked in and could see it was a bad, bad place. I see all these guys laying on the bar. I walked in."

No, he didn't just walk in. Joe Pepitone had an announcement to make.

"I say, 'I'm Joe Pepitone of the New York Yankees. I'm supposed to meet Mr. Whitey Ford and Mr. Mi ckey Mantle here.' People just looked at me. One guy says, 'You better get out of here before you get yourselves killed.' We realize they played a joke on us. So we take another cab back for another $35.

"I tell Phil, 'Listen, when we get on the bus to go to the ballpark tomorrow, let me do the talking.' Just as I get on, I see Mickey in the back and I say, 'Mickey, I couldn't get there last night with Phil. I had to come home and call my mother.' He says, 'You're full of crap. We saw you there. We were sitting in the back. We saw you come in.' He was full of crap. They just sent us on a wild goose-chase. That's what they used to do."

Hair Today, Gone Tomorrow

When Joe Pepitone started going bald, he would use two hairpieces, a large toupee for wear in the public and a smaller one when he had to wear his baseball cap. He also took to carrying a small hairdressing kit with him wherever he went to tend to his natural hair.

The small bag always had a hot comb, different greases, a hairdryer and glue for the hairpieces.

During one game, Fritz Peterson and Jim Bouton decided to play a little trick on Pepitone. Sneaking into the clubhouse, the pair filled Pepitone's hairdryer with talcum powder. After

Joe Pepitone

a particularly tough loss, Pepitone came out of the shower and turned on the dryer. Within seconds he was covered in powder.

Loss or not, it broke up the entire clubhouse.

Burnin' It Up

Pepitone was giving a hot-foot (secretly sticking fired matches on someone's shoe) to one of his teammates one day not realizing that Phil Linz was doing the same to him.

One moment he was smirking in delight, the next he was hopping around the dugout trying to put his own flames out.

Incommunicado?

Pepitone never lived down a throwing error, which cost the Yankees a victory in the 1963 World Series.

A year later, back in the Fall Classic, Pepitone actually shook off a pick-off sign by pitcher Jim Bouton.

"He was standing there shaking his head, tiny shakes because he didn't want anybody to see," Bouton said. "It was the first time I ever saw anybody shake off a pick-off sign.

"Just for the hell of it, I gave him the sign again a few pitches later. I wanted to see if he'd shake me off again. He did."

GAYLORD PERRY

Billboard?

A lasting image of Gaylord Perry is the uniform he used to wear to some Old-Timer's Games. It's unique in that the logos of every team he played for are emblazoned somewhere on the shirt. There are race cars with fewer emblems on board.

The Wet One

Since Perry has played with so many teams, there were few players who didn't learn of his spit-ball techniques, not that they found a way to hit the spitter either. "You know the situations when he's going to throw you a spitter," Yankee third baseman Graig Nettles said, "and you know it's coming, but it's still a very hard pitch to hit."

Greasy Kid's Stuff

Perry often placed Vaseline on areas of his uniform. Before he'd go into his windup he'd be touching his neck or his belt or his hat, planting the thought into the batter's head that he was "greasing up" even if he wasn't.

Another neat trick involved Perry's use of the rosin bag. He'd pick it up and flip it in his hand a few times before setting it down.

When he released the next pitch a puff of rosin would appear.

FRITZ PETERSON

Fast Cats

Jim Bouton and Fritz Peterson were perfect roommates for one another, even if Ralph Houk tried to split them up one spring.

They used to race cars down the California coastline, playing loud Spanish music along the way. Their trips to San Francisco always included a run past the hippies in the public parks.

Bouton was telling Peterson one day about how he thrived on nervous tension to pitch better.

So before Bouton's next start, Peterson came up to Bouton and whispered in his ear: "If you want to see your baby again you'll win today."

KEN PHELPS

So Do How Does it Feel to be the Punchline?

The 1988 trade of Jay Buhner for Ken Phelps was immortalized on 'Seinfeld' when the character played by Jerry Stiller excoriates 'George Steinbrenner' saying, "How could you trade Jay Buhner?"

"To me, I have kind of learned to laugh it off. It's more important to be remembered for something than to not be remembered at all. I think I got more publicity coming off of that 'Seinfeld' episode than any other thing I did in my career. It was amazing how many people watched that and still talk about that today. But I learned to let it bounce off. At the time, it was a little bit upsetting. I had roots in Seattle and I was having a big year there and when I got over to New York I kind of got lost in the shuffle a little bit. I think I probably would have had my best year ever in baseball had I stayed in Seattle in '88. The way George Argyros, the owner of the Mariners, was doing things in those years, he was trying to unload people if their salaries were getting a little bit too high. He was never fixing what was wrong with that ballclub. He was always getting rid of the guys who were doing well and it wasn't that long afterward that they got rid of Mark Langston and Alvin Davis and cleaned house."

Oh, You Must be Number 21

Ken Phelps' stay in New York, on a personal level, was cloaked in anonymity.

"I got over to New York and there wasn't anybody there other than the players to greet me. After the trade, I never spoke to George Steinbrenner. It wasn't, 'Hey, welcome to the Yankees' or anything like that. I never heard it from him."

It's not as if it cost him anything to say hello.

"I never got any of his money. I never got any Yankee money. I come over there on the last year of a Mariner contract. I played there and then I remember in spring training in '89, I had hit a home run against the Orioles down in Miami that won the game that night. They gave me off the next day. I was in the locker room getting ready to go out to the bench just before the game. Steinbrenner was on the other side of the room with a couple of friends of his. I heard a voice from the other side of the room say, 'Hey, Phelps.' I hadn't spoken to Steinbrenner so I kind of looked that way. I didn't think it was him. Sure enough, it was him. He said, 'Hey, Phelps.' I turn and look at him and he says, 'Looks like you're finally getting your swing.' I said, 'Yeah, yeah, it's coming around, it feels pretty good.'"

And that is all George Steinbrenner ever said to Ken Phelps in the year-and-a-half that he was there. He was traded to the Oakland As and received a World Series ring in 1989, seven years before George Steinbrenner did again.

LOU PINIELLA

Set The Alarm, Grab The Bat

Hitting was a science for Lou Piniella. He'd practice his swing whenever possible, even in the middle of the night. Piniella gave up tossing and turning in bed one evening to work on a new batting stance. Using a bat he kept near his bed, Piniella was taking a couple practice swings when he was shocked by a scream. It was his wife, Anita, who had opened her eyes only to see a man standing over her swinging a bat.

"I could hardly blame her for the shriek," a sheepish Piniella said.

It was a rare day when Yankee teammates didn't spot Piniella practicing his swing in front of a mirror in the clubhouse.

Graig Nettles liked to poke fun at Piniella and his protege Roy Smalley.

"This is Leonard Nimoy along with Lou Piniella and Roy Smalley, 'In search of... the Perfect Swing.'"

Smashing Porcelain (And Other Cracks)

Baseball players have often shown little or no regard for the amenities and equipment offered for their comfort, especially after a particularly bad outing.

Lou Piniella

For Lou Piniella, water coolers were usually the target of his outrage. Billy Martin had a penchant for smashing urinals.

At old Cleveland Stadium, there's a long walkway from the dugout to the visitor's clubhouse. After the Indians put up a six-spot in the first inning, Martin not only smashed out all the lights in the runway but also demolished another urinal.

Piniella was never one to pass up a good one-liner so he offered this. "I'm going to go out there tomorrow with a flashlight taped to my helmet so I can get back up to the clubhouse after the game."

Piniella let his temper get the best of him in the 1976 season. A home plate scrap with Boston Red Sox catcher Carlton Fisk resulted in bruised tendons and ligaments in Piniella's hand.

Weeks later, as the hand was just about healed up, a rough outing at the plate sent Piniella into a clubhouse rage. His misdirected attempt at smashing a stool against the wall found his hand slipping in between.

Nice 'N' Neat, You Hear?

George Steinbrenner was always a stickler for neatness. He dressed well and he wanted his players to look appropriate as well.

One spring training Lou Piniella showed up in camp with long hair. Clubhouse manager Pete Sheehy told Piniella he wasn't allowed to dress and was instructed to report to Steinbrenner's trailer office.

Piniella and Steinbrenner had the following conversation.

"Lou, you can't dress with hair that long."

"Why not? What has long hair to do with my ability to play?"

"It's a matter of discipline. I just won't have it."

The argument continued.

Said Piniella: "If our Lord, Jesus Christ, came back down with his long hair, you wouldn't let him play on this team."

Steinbrenner got out of his chair and had Piniella follow him across the street to a pool in the back of a motel. "If you can walk across the water in that pool," Steinbrenner said, "you don't have to get a haircut."

Point made. Piniella reported the next day with a nice and appropriate haircut.

Managing Just Fine

George Steinbrenner thought Lou Piniella would make a great manager someday so, in his usual course of taking action before thinking, he decided to make that point public.

Of course, Steinbrenner already had a manager in place—Billy Martin—but with that tumultuous relationship it was probably best to have an ace up your sleeve.

Piniella got his first crack at managing the Yankees on an interim basis in July 1985. Martin had to be hospitalized when a doctor accidentally punctured his lung while trying to administer a muscle relaxant shot for Martin's aching back.

Steinbrenner phoned Piniella in Texas, where the Yankees were just finishing up a series with the Rangers, and told Piniella he would be taking over the club for a few days. To Piniella's dismay, Steinbrenner neglected to call Martin first, so Billy had to hear the news from someone else.

The club flew to Ohio, and Piniella arrived at Cleveland Stadium early the next day to assume duties. He was informed by coach Doug Holmquist that Martin had called the clubhouse already and would have the lineup phoned in within an hour. The problems began when Piniella made his first mistake by failing to make out a lineup card—he thought coach Gene Michael did that since he always posted it for the players.

Martin kept in touch with Piniella via the telephone from his hospital bed in Arlington, Texas. With injured catcher Butch Wynegar serving as phone operator for a night, Martin called in each of the first three innings just to get updates and query Piniella on a few things. When the press caught wind of this after the game, their stories told of how Martin managed the Yankees from his hospital bed.

The Yankees won the first two games under the Piniella/ Martin setup and then lost three. Prank phone callers tied up the phone line in the Yankees dugout, pretending to be Steinbrenner or Martin, infuriating the latter when his real calls couldn't get through. Players started questioning Piniella's moves. A fan yelled from the stands, " Is that your decision or is it coming from a hospital bed in Texas?"

By the end of the Indians series, Piniella was so flustered he took a souvenir baseball from his first win as manager and threw it into a urinal in the clubhouse.

"I had been made to look foolish on the field and in the dugout," Piniella fumed.

When he got home to New York, he told his wife he was quitting baseball altogether. However, calmer heads prevailed.

Steinbrenner and Martin both asked Piniella to return as hitting coach.

TIM RAINES

I Went to a Fight and a Baseball Game Broke Out

All hell broke loose inside Yankee Stadium one night in 1998 when Armando Benitez of the Orioles hit Tino Martinez square in the back with a 98 mile-per-hour fastball on the first pitch after he gave up a pivotal home run to Bernie Williams.

"The benches emptied and a big fight broke out. It seemed to go on for an hour. Both benches had cleared and the fight drifted into the Baltimore dugout."

Tim Raines was the next guy up. Benitez was ejected, replaced by Bobby Munoz, the ex-Yankee once billboarded years earlier with so much promise.

"The first pitch I saw, I hit it over the right-centerfield wall. I think that was sort of like payback to the Orioles for them hitting Tino. The crowd just went crazy. I think that moment and that at-bat sticks out more than just about anything I did in New York."

In 21st century baseball where, seemingly, at one time or another, everybody plays with everybody else at one time or another, Bobby Munoz and Tim Raines were teammates in 2001 with the Montreal Expos.

Tim Raines

WILLIE RANDOLPH

The Home Show

With Yankee Stadium playing host to its third All-Star Game in 1977, New York City product Willie Randolph made sure it was a special night in the Big Apple.

The starting second baseman collected a run-producing single. "I was a young kid in front of my hometown fans, my family," Randolph said. "I played the whole game. I was there playing with guys I had grown up idolizing—Rod Carew, Reggie Jackson."

ALLIE REYNOLDS

Historic Stuff

Allie Reynolds secured his place in history in 1951 as the first American League pitcher to hurl two no-hitters in the same season. On July 12, he won a 1-0 duel with former roommate Bob Feller of the Cleveland Indians, facing only 29 batters.

On September 28, the Yankees beat up on the Boston Red Sox, 8-0, only a funny thing happened on the way to his second no-no.

Ted Williams had wrapped up his 10th consecutive season of hitting over .300 and now stood in the way of Reynolds' glory.

Down 0-1 in the count, Williams fouled a fastball high behind home plate. Catcher Yogi Berra got under it, but failed to make the catch.

Reynolds helped Berra to his feet and said, "Don't worry Yogi, we'll get him next time."

Williams shot back at Berra. "You blew it. You son of a bitches put me in a hell of a spot. Now I've got to bear down even harder even though the game is decided and your man has a no-hitter going."

As far as Berra was concerned, the pitch almost worked once, it should again. Sure enough, a fastball was fouled off in the direction of the Yankee dugout and this time Berra made the grab to complete the no-hitter and the 1951 pennant clincher.

DAVE RIGHETTI

2003 Makes it 20 Years

Nineteen eighty-three was the first full year Dave Righetti
was getting the ball. And he got it on Independence
Day to start against Boston at the Stadium. The result
was the Yankees' first regular-season no-hitter in 32 years.

"There were so many little side-plots that happened that day
that I didn't realize until I was done because nobody talked
to you. Nettles couldn't play because he had pink eye and he
couldn't go outside. Willie Randolph didn't play either. Andre
Robertson played second base. Donnie played first but at that
time, he wasn't playing there fulltime. So we had some different
people out there."

There was a reason for the substitutions.

"They had beaten us up for three straight days. I think maybe
Billy decided to get to the All-Star break like, 'Let's just get out
of here, rest up and go get them in the second half.'"

Righetti was too young to recognize he had something special
warming up in the bullpen.

"At that age, I felt pretty good all the time. That was long
before I started wearing my arm out. It was strange. I had
trouble all day. I was throwing very hard that day, no question.
Even my slider wasn't really going down. Occasionally it did,
but it was really a hard one and stayed on the waist a lot, which

is unusually high. I couldn't get it down because I was throwing it so hard. So I decided to use it more as cutter and I ran the ball underneath their hands instead of that down-and-in-the-dirt slider that Gator and Sparky had used all the time, something I was trying to perfect at that time."

Righetti, then, had just the one pitch effectively, his fastball.

"I had just pitched against those guys the start before in Boston. I was using all my pitches. I think I threw just one change-up, I might not have thrown one curveball, I threw all fastballs."

That command was missing in New York.

"In this game, I really didn't have great control. I just had this ball that was jumping around so I just stuck with it. I didn't force that slider down. Normally I would. I just let it go and it landed where it landed."

Of all the gin joints in the world, she had to walk into this one. Of all the hitters in the world, Wade Boggs stood between Dave Righetti and immortality.

"He was very hot. I think he was hitting .360-something. The last thing I thought about was striking him out. Twice during the game he hit balls to centerfield. I used to knock him down all the time, including that last at-bat. I always threw the ball in on him as hard as I could and just let him spray it off to the left. I'd get an easy strike and try to get him to at least give up on the plate a little bit and then use the slider on him. But I couldn't get the darn thing down and away to him. So I just used fastballs on him and Jerry Remy, who was also giving me trouble. On the last pitch, Butch Wynegar called for a slider and that was the right pitch. I had knocked him down and he had been frozen twice on pitches away already but Steve Palermo hadn't called it. I said, 'Well, I have to get this one down somehow.' I was tired enough I think that it went down. I aimed right in the ground when I threw it. I don't think it hit the ground. I think Butch caught it in the air. That is my recollection. I just went, 'Geez, thank God this is over.'"

Dave Righetti

Race? What Race? Just Wake Me Up When It's Over

On the final day of the 1984 season, Don Mattingly and Dave Winfield staged their fight-to-the-finish showdown for the American League batting title. The Detroit Tigers, on their way to a World Championship, provided the weekend's opposition at the Stadium. Dave Righetti remembers something else from that final Sunday.

"Willie Hernandez is warming up for them which seemed odd given the circumstances. There was a van in center field that was used back then to ferry the relief pitchers into the game. It had a big Yankee emblem on the side. When they opened the double gates, the van would be sitting right there."

On this day, Bob Shirley was asleep in the front seat... just as Sparky Anderson went to the mound and made the motion for Hernandez.

"He's just snoring away and Hernandez is banging on the window yelling at him in Spanish. Shirley wakes up and goes, 'Hey, what's up?' The umpires are standing out there waiting for this van to start and bring him in. Well, Bob Shirley, instead of getting out and letting the regular guy drive in, he jumps over to the driver's seat and drives the van in with Hernandez."

In uniform.

"He drives the van around to the front of their dugout, slams on the brakes and there's rocks flying everywhere. Hernandez gets out and Shirley takes off and gives that smart-aleck little wave he used to do.

"I wished I was down there but I was down in the bullpen."

MICKEY RIVERS

T he beloved John Milton Rivers, aka The Gozzlehead, once explained his philosophy of life to a New York writer as follows:

"Ain't no sense worrying about things you have control over, 'cause if you got control over them ain't no sense worrying. And ain't no sense worrying about things you got no control over, 'cause if you got no control over them, ain't no sense worrying about them."

Of course.

The above is official. It was made so in the 1982 Texas Rangers press guide, of which Rivers was a member.

Pushing the Gozzlehead's Buttons So He Can Hear These Magic Words: And They're Off!

It's September, 1978 and the Yankees have just arrived in Boston for an off-the-charts series of importance. The word 'massacre' is not yet on anyone's lips. Jay Johnstone says it's time to assuage the team's sparkplug and his love for horseplay, literally.

Mickey Rivers

"It all started when a bunch of us got together. There was Piniella, Nettles, Jim Spencer, Fred Stanley, myself and one other guy. We got Mickey Rivers in the coffee shop of the Sheraton Boston about 10:30 in the morning before the first game. I lockered next to Mickey and knew him from our days together in the Angels organization."

The Gang of Six gave him a talking to...gently.

"We explained to him in order for us to win the division and possibly get to the next level, he needed to get on base. And if he got on base for us as our leadoff hitter and the catalyst for our team, we would probably net about $10,000. And if we netted about $10,000 per man, do you know how many horses you can bet on?"

Mickey's eyes lit up.

"He kept going, '$10,000?' 'Yeah, Mickey, if we win we're getting $10,000. Do you know how much fun you can have at the track?'

"Mickey Rivers was 3-for-3 in the first game before Butch Hobson, the ninth-place hitter for the Sox, came to bat once. He went on to get, I forget exactly how many that series, something like 11 hits. We went on to score about 49 runs on 67 hits or something like that. We beat them four in a row and that's what turned it around."

A gallant comeback that stretched over a 14-game deficit was almost complete.

And He Means It, Too

Mickey Rivers was the answer to the Yankees' base-running needs when he was acquired from the Texas Rangers in 1976.

Mick the Quick stole 93 bases over four seasons, 43 in his first season in pinstripes. However, to look at him, it seemed as though his legs were always pained as he took a slow walk to the home-plate circle.

Rivers was a carefree spirit who didn't let things bother him. Consider:

"Ain't no sense worrying about things you got control over, 'cause if you got control over them, ain't no sense in worrying. And there ain't no sense worrying about things you got no control over, 'cause if you got no control over them, ain't no sense worrying."

Happy Together

Marital disharmony cost Rivers dearly one afternoon. After spending a night away from home, Rivers was greeted at Yankee Stadium by his wife.

Several times, she plowed the Mercedes she was driving into the Cadillac he had taken to the ballpark. Then she slapped him around a few times in the parking lot before going home and burning all his clothes. He was forced to wear sweatsuits for more than a week.

Bet The Field

Mickey Rivers enjoyed going to the racetrack, even if his teammates were convinced he was the worst handicapper around.

"He would study those charts night and day," Lou Piniella said, "devour the *Racing Form* and pick nothing but losers. It got to be a joke."

Rivers would pick one way, and everyone with him would go the other way, Piniella said.

On one trip to Thistledown outside Cleveland, Rivers told Piniella that he had picked the winner of the sixth race and was banking $20 on the horse. Sure enough, Rivers' horse won and he cashed in. It was only later that Rivers admitted he had bet $20 on every horse in the race.

"Had to have a winner, Lou," he said. "Had to have it. Had to break my luck."

Phil Rizzuto

Taller Than He Appeared

Phil Rizzuto stood only 5 feet, 6 inches tall, but there was no better shortstop in his era. Casey Stengel's "little fella" was the American League leader in double plays three times. Same goes for total chances. Said starting pitcher Vic Raschi: "My best pitch is anything the batter grounds, lines or pops in the direction of Rizzuto."

Welcome, Stranger!

Phil Rizzuto was not welcomed to the Yankees with open arms.

Nixed by Casey Stengel in a tryout with the Brooklyn Dodgers, the Yankees liked what they saw in the Brooklynite and signed him to a minor league deal in 1937. Four seasons later he was up with the big club, only established veteran Frank Crosetti was patrolling the left side of the infield. Several veterans made it tough on Rizzuto to even get batting cage time until Joe DiMaggio came to the kid's rescue.

Phil Rizzuto

Step On A Crack...

Phil Rizzuto was as superstitious as any player. He had to step out of bed on the same side every morning. He would never step on a baseline. He even had a great fear of insects.

Add One Stick Of Butter

Phil Rizzuto went right from the playing field to the broadcaster's booth upon retirement. He never stopped being a fan favorite, thanks to the charm he showed during his broadcasts.

He liked to keep things light when he could, sharing recipes over the air or running off a list of birthday wishes.

Holy !@#$

Phil Rizzuto was honored at Yankee Stadium on many occasions, but none as funny as a summer day in 1985.

The Chicago White Sox were visiting with none other than former New York Mets standout and future Hall of Famer Tom Seaver going for victory 300 (which he got in a gem of an outing). Rizzuto should have known the day wasn't quite his when the cow the club gave him—in honor of his broadcast call "Holy Cow"—stepped on his foot.

A Hall-mark

Admission to the Pro Baseball Hall of Fame was a long time coming for Rizzuto, who was finally voted in on February 25, 1994.

"I said, 'Holy Cow' and almost fell to the floor," he said. "I never gave up about the Hall of Fame as long as I was eligible and still breathing."

CHARLES "RED" RUFFING

We'll Show You

The Boston Red Sox obviously didn't learn their lesson when they traded 22-game loser Charles "Red" Ruffing to the Yankees following the 1929 season.

Not only could Ruffing hit (his 520 hits ranks him third best in history for a pitcher), he could pitch. In 15 seasons with the Yankees, Ruffing posted only one losing season. The right-hander played in seven World Series and posted a 7-2 record. He was voted into the Pro Baseball Hall of Fame in 1967.

Not bad for a man who lost four toes on his left foot in a mining accident years earlier.

BABE RUTH

Did You Know?

How did Babe Ruth get his nickname, Bambino? From the Italian neighborhoods. Babe is translated to "Bambino" in Italian.

After The Game

Babe Ruth's success on the field was only matched by his legendary lifestyle as a carouser and womanizer.

Writer Lee Allen described Ruth as "a large man in a camel's hair coat and camel's hair cap, standing in front of a hotel, his broad nostrils sniffing at the promise of the night."

When it wasn't time for baseball, it was time for having fun. Ruth was rarely seen in the hotels the club frequented, unless he was cavorting with the women of his choice.

Sometimes Ruth would go out looking for fun as soon as the team train pulled into town.

Outfielder Frank "Ping" Bodie was not only Ruth's roommate on the road but also his luggage carrier, it seems. All the players' bags were usually delivered to the hotel lobby, from where the players would pick up their belongings and bring

Babe Ruth

them to their rooms. Since Ruth was rarely around for that drill, the dutiful Bodie would lug Ruth's bags to the room for him.

One day a reporter asked Bodie what Ruth was like when he and Bodie were alone.

"I don't know anything about him," Bodie said. The incredulous reporter rephrased the question, but to no satisfaction.

"I don't room with him," Bodie said. "I room with his suitcase."

Some Start

Babe Ruth played 2,120 games in the Yankee pinstripes. While many were memorable, his debut in 1920 was not.

Manager Miller Huggins had Ruth play center field since "Ping" Bodie had left the team during spring training and Chick Fewster was hit in the head with a pitch and left speechless for weeks. Ruth dropped a fly ball in the eighth inning with two men on base and two outs, allowing the host Philadelphia A's to win.

The next day, a messenger interrupted play (something not uncommon in those days) and handed Ruth a package. Inside was a shabby brown derby purchased by Philadelphia third baseman Joe Dugan, the recipient of the "gift" play a day earlier.

Amidst the laughter of players and the crowd, Ruth smiled and donned the derby.

It would be another two weeks before Ruth finally hit his first home run as a Yankee. On May 1, Ruth belted a shot far over the roof at the Polo Grounds for his first of 659 regular-season homers in pinstripes.

Big Bat

Babe Ruth's first two years as a Yankee were two of his best. In 1920 he batted .376, hit 54 home runs (when 28 was his previous major league record) and drove in 137 runs. In 1921 he batted .378 with 59 homers and 171 RBIs.

It's clear Ruth had the upper hand in negotiating his next contract with Yankee management. An offer of $30,000 with bonus clauses was rejected. So too was a $40,000 offer. The Yankees finally proposed $50,000 for five years. It still wasn't enough.

"Make it $52,000," Ruth said. "There are 52 weeks in the year, and I've always wanted to make a grand a week."

In 1930, Ruth was only hours away from holding out—possibly for the season—after stalled contract talks. Finally, Ruth and co-owner Colonel Jacob Ruppert agreed to a two-year deal at $80,000 per.

It is said that when someone told Ruth that he was making $5,000 more than President Herbert Hoover, Ruth said, "Why not? I had a better year than he did."

Major Consumer

The story of Babe Ruth once eating a dozen hot dogs before a game is untrue, but the Bambino could really put the food away when he wanted to.

Frank "Ping" Bodie roomed with Ruth for two seasons. The 5-foot-8, 195-pound Bodie was championed as the team's biggest eater—that is, until Ruth came along.

"Anybody who eats three pounds of steak and a bottle of chili sauce for a starter has got me beat," Bodie said.

Act II

The diamond wasn't the only stage Babe Ruth performed upon. Starting in the fall of 1921, Ruth earned $3,000 per week on a 16-week vaudeville tour of the Northeast. Actually, the critics were fairly kind to Ruth, who demonstrated his baritone voice and his comic delivery.

Close Call

Babe Ruth had a penchant for fast cars. Speed limits and traffic signs meant little to Ruth, who had little difficulty talking his way out of traffic tickets due to his fame.

During his second season as a Yankee, a police officer—unconvinced or unimpressed with who Ruth was—arrested Ruth for speeding on Riverside Drive. Not only did Ruth pay the $100 fine, he was sentenced to a day in jail. Back then, "a day" ended at 4 p.m., so Ruth was happy he wouldn't have to miss all of that afternoon's 3:15 p.m. start.

Ruth had his uniform delivered to the jailhouse in lower Manhattan and put it on underneath his fine suit. Not heeding any advice from the judge, Ruth told someone in his jail cell, "I'm going to have to go like hell to get to the game. Keeping you late like this makes you into a speeder."

At four o'clock Ruth was released, and a crowd greeted him at the rear of the jail. This time, utilizing a police escort, Ruth made it to the ballpark in the upper half of Manhattan in 18 minutes and was inserted into the lineup.

A year earlier, in July 1920, Ruth was driving his four-door touring sedan from Washington, D.C., back to New York following a ballgame. Joining Ruth on the trip was his wife, Helen, outfielder Frank Gleich, backup catcher Fred Hofmann and coach Charley O'Leary.

While driving through Wawa, Pennsylvania, Ruth was driving too fast and failed to negotiate a curve. Ruth hit the brakes, but not soon enough to prevent the sedan from skidding off the road and flipping over. Charley O'Leary and Helen Ruth were the only passengers thrown from the vehicle, Ruth onto soft dirt and O'Leary onto the road's hard surface.

Babe thought he had killed O'Leary, who lay motionless. Ruth raised O'Leary's head and said, "Speak to me, Charley." O'Leary shook off his grogginess and demanded to know where his brand-new straw hat was.

All five passengers walked to a farmhouse where they stayed overnight. The next day they read a newspaper headline that trumpeted, "RUTH REPORTED KILLED IN CAR CRASH."

A Huh of Activity

Whenever a new pitcher served up a home run to Ruth, the Yankee would bellow in laughter about adding another to the growing list. It's not often any pitcher got the best of Ruth, save for one young left-hander named Hub Pruett.

Hurling for the St. Louis Browns, the 21-year-old Pruett struck out Ruth in their first meeting in May 1922. A month later, Pruett fanned Ruth again in a relief outing. Two days later, Pruett rang Ruth up three times in a starting role.

In a July matchup, Pruett induced a weak grounder back to the mound and fanned Ruth three more times. In August, a sore-armed Pruett answered the call in relief by striking out Ruth with the bases loaded.

A September meeting yielded a walk and another strikeout, the 10th in 14 plate appearances for Ruth. Finally, Ruth homered off Pruett in their 15th encounter. Ruth added three more strikeouts, a walk and a home run in the first five plate appearances against Pruett in 1923. Even though Pruett fanned Ruth only once more, he had retired the Babe on strikes 13 times in their first 21 face-to-face outings.

Pruett used his baseball earnings (he pitched for 10 seasons) to put himself through medical school. Dr. Pruett met up with Ruth many years later.

"I want to thank you for putting me through med school," Pruett said. "If it wasn't for you, no one would have heard of me." Ruth just smiled and said, "If I helped you get through medical school, I'm glad of it."

The Real Story Is ...

The story about Babe Ruth hitting a home run for a dying child was stretched somewhat.

In fact, an 11-year-old boy named Johnny Sylvester was hospitalized after being thrown off a horse.

A friend of the family had baseballs signed by the St. Louis Cardinals and New York Yankees and Ruth promised he would hit a home run during the World Series (he hit four).

After the Series, Ruth paid a hospital visit to the thrilled little boy.

Called Shot?

The most disputed legend of Babe Ruth is his called home run shot in the 1932 World Series. The Yankees won two games in the Bronx by scores of 12-6 and 5-2. There was considerable taunting between the two teams, a fact the Chicago sportswriters pointed out in their stories.

That only raised the fervor of Cubs fans when the series moved to Wrigley Field.

Charlie Root got the Game Three start for the Cubs but was rudely welcomed by the Yankees. Shortstop Billy Jurges threw away the first grounder by Earle Combs, and Root walked Joe Sewell.

Ruth had already hit nine home runs during batting practice, and the fans greeted him with a chorus of boos. Having already pointed to the right-field bleachers before his at-bat, Ruth knocked a 2-0 fastball to that very spot. But there was more to come.

The Cubs rescued Root with some runs, tying the game at 4-4 in the fourth as Ruth misplayed a ball into a double. Most of the Cubs players were on the top of the dugout steps razzing Ruth as he stepped to the plate in the fifth. Root received a called strike. Ruth casually raised one finger. Following two balls, Root again got a called strike.

This time Ruth waved the Cubs players back into their dugout and raised two fingers. Root jawed with Ruth, who shouted back and gestured toward the hurler (which many people claim was Ruth pointing to centerfield). The next pitch was a change-up breaking down and away from Ruth, but the hitter reached down and deposited the ball deep into the seats in center for the longest home run in Wrigley history.

The Yankees won Game Three, 7-5, and Game Four, 13-6.

Actually, his first called home run in a World Series took place four years earlier, in 1928, against the St. Louis Cardinals. The Yankees had swept the first three games handily before the Cardinals put up a fight in Game Four.

Ruth homered in the fourth inning to tie the game at 1-1. Trailing 2-1 heading into the seventh, left-hander Willie Sherdel got two strikes on Ruth and tried quick-pitching Ruth while the hitter had his head turned while talking to catcher Earl Smith.

In the National League, quick pitches were allowed, but this was World Series play and it was agreed to beforehand by the league presidents that this would not be allowed. The Cardinals argued in vain while Ruth smiled from outside the batter's box. Ruth clapped when the argument ceased and exchanged words with Sherdel.

After two balls were issued, Ruth told Sherdel, "Put one right here and I'll knock it out of the park for you."

Sure enough, Sherdel did and Ruth deposited the ball into the right-field seats.

A Kind Gesture

The bat Babe Ruth used to hit his 50th home run in 1920 (he finished with 54) was auctioned off with proceeds going to help starving Armenians in Turkey.

Aware that people wanted a piece of history, Ruth trotted around the bases with the bat that produced his 56th home run in 1927.

A boy came out of the stands, patted Ruth on the back and grabbed the bat. Ruth carried the boy and the bat across home plate.

Don't Even Try It

Seven hundred and fourteen home runs is an incredible figure, but it was wrong to try to cheat Ruth of a blast.

Tom Zachary served up home run number 60 to Ruth on September 30, 1927. Ruth poked a shot down the right-field line. Zachary argued the ball was foul to the umpire, but received no satisfaction.

Twenty years later, Zachary and Ruth met at Yankee Stadium. Ruth looked at him and said in a croaky voice, "You crooked-arm son of a bitch, are you still claiming that ball was foul?"

He Could Pitch, Too

Babe Ruth was a standout pitcher for the Boston Red Sox, but the Yankees frowned on using Ruth on the hill.

In 2,084 regular-season games with the Yankees, Ruth played first base 14 times and pitched on five occasions. He was 2-0 in 1920, 1-0 in 1921, 1930 and 1933.

For The Record

A common misnomer has the Baby Ruth candy bar named after the home run champ. In fact, the chocolate bar was named after President Grover Cleveland's daughter, Ruth, who was born in the White House.

A patent fight eventually did away with a chocolate bar that was named after him: Babe Ruth's Home Run Candy.

In fact, presidential protocol was lost on Ruth. On a very hot day at the ballpark in Washington, D.C., Ruth was heard to tell President Warren Harding, "Hot as hell, ain't it, Prez?"

Proving Them Wrong

Americans like to build up their heroes and just as quickly tear them down. Babe Ruth was to learn this during a troubled 1925 season.

During an exhibition tour following spring training, Ruth developed an intestinal abscess, the result of not taking care of himself, his doctor told him.

A 20-minute surgical procedure did the trick, but Ruth was never quite the same that season. He batted .290 and hit only 25 home runs in 98 games.

Writer Fred Lieb wrote Ruth off in an August piece.

"It is doubtful that Ruth again will be the superstar that he was from 1919 through 1924."

He went on to write how Ruth should be able to produce 30 home runs or so and a dependable .325 average for a couple years.

Ruth would average 50 home runs and hit over .350 in four of the next six seasons.

True Love

Babe Ruth christened the 1929 season by marrying his second wife, Claire, in a 6 a.m. ceremony on the day of the opener. The afternoon contest was eventually rained out, so Claire made her first Yankee Stadium appearance as Babe's wife the next day. Sure enough, Babe hit a home run and tipped his hat to her as he rounded third base.

Heartfelt

The Yankees held a Babe Ruth Day at Yankee Stadium on April 27, 1947, more than a year before his death. The following was his raspy speech:

"Thank you very much, ladies and gentlemen. You know how bad my voice sounds. Well it feels just as bad. You know, this baseball game of ours comes up from the youth. That means the boys. And after you're a boy and grow up to play ball, then you come to the boys you see representing clubs today in your national pastime. The only real game in the world, I think, is baseball.

"As a rule, people think that if you give boys a football or a baseball or something like that, they naturally become athletes right away. But you can't do that in baseball. You've got to start from way down, at the bottom, when the boys are six or seven years of age. You can't wait until they're 15 or 16. You've got to let it grow up with you, if you're the boy. And if you try hard enough, you're bound to come out on top, just as these boys here have come to the top now.

"There have been so many lovely things said about me today, that I'm glad to have had the opportunity to thank everybody. Thank you."

Pour One More

Babe Ruth succumbed to cancer, at age 53, on August 16, 1948. His body lay in state at the main entrance of Yankee Stadium for two days, during which time more than 100,000 people passed his coffin. His funeral was attended by more than 7,000 people.

Pallbearer Joe Dugan made light of the weighty hero's casket. "I'd give $100 for an ice cold beer," he said. Noted pallbearer Waite Hoyt, "So would the Babe."

A Little Extra Dough

Barnstorming tours were an avenue for baseball players to make some cash in the weeks following a season.

Early in Ruth's career, he could command $1,500 for appearing in an exhibition contest. Following the 1920 season, Ruth joined a group of New York Giants on a barnstorming tour of Cuba where he reportedly made $40,000.

What's a player to do with all that money except gamble it away? Ruth enjoyed going to the horse track in Havana. He didn't particularly enjoy losing money, though. On one race Ruth lost $25,000. By trip's end, Babe's wife, Helen, had to buy the tickets for the boat trip home.

BILLY SAMPLE

Barely a Need to Shower

illy Sample wore an albatross when he was active, the label of part-time player. So imagine his excitement when he showed up and found his name in Billy Martin's starting line-up, playing left field, for the 1985 Yankees.

"I was in Baltimore and had singled in a run in my first at-bat. The bases were loaded and I'm up again. Except this time, Ken Griffey Sr. pinch-hit for me."

In the second inning.

"I laugh now when I think about getting pinch-hit for in the second inning but I kind of understood it. It had never happened before. If I had to be pinch-hit for by anybody, I could accept being pinch-hit for by somebody as talented as Ken Griffey Sr., a .296 lifetime hitter. As it turned it, Senior came through with a base-hit."

Sample had heard worse, though.

"Oscar Gamble, when he was with Texas, was already in the batter's box. And he wound up being their leading hitter before that aborted trade to the Yankees in '79. There was a whistle from the dugout and there he was walking back. I guess it can happen to anybody. You certainly would hope that your manager has the decorum and the courtesy and the respect for you to do it as early as possible and not wait until you get in the batter's box."

No HBP

Prior to coming to the Yankees, Billy Sample played half a dozen seasons in Texas, where Billy Martin once managed.

In 1983, Martin was managing the Yankees who were playing a spring training game against the Rangers in Pom-pano Beach, Florida, a game he was taking way too seriously.

"When I was broadcasting with the Braves and Goose was with the Padres. I wasn't big on talking to the opposing players when I played.

"But I could tell that he wanted to say something to me. We finally met in San Diego under the stands and he asked, 'How did you and Billy Martin get along?' I said, 'Well, he didn't like me, but I didn't dislike him.' I asked him why he would ask. He said that while shagging flies in the outfield before a game, Billy told him to hit me in the head."

Gossage refused to carry out Martin's wishes.

"He said he thought it hurt his relationship with Billy because he didn't do it. He didn't know if Billy was testing him."

Sample knew nothing about it.

"Goose said he could have killed me and I wouldn't have known it. I was so young then, he would have split the helmet, go down to first and not think anything about it."

Rafael Santana

Robin Ventura is the 69th person to have played for both local teams. He is only the latest player from the left side of the Mets infield to cross the Triborough Bridge and head up the Major Deegan Expressway to his new home.

"It was an honor to play for both teams. When I found out I was going to the Yankees, my heart was in New York. I loved the fans. They appreciated what I did there."

Geographically, it wasn't far

"It was a different atmosphere. Over at Shea Stadium with the Mets, after playing many years with the same guys, it kind of made you feel like you were at home. When I got traded to the Yankees, I went over there and had to meet new people and deal with a different front office. But I was able to make my adjustment and have fun while I was there. So I don't think it was a big deal for me to move from one side to the other one."

Being There

No one highlight or moment resonates inside Rafael Santana's memory bank as a Yankee. Just the totality of the experience at the holy of holies.

"I think the biggest highlight with the Yankees was being able to play at the place where some many superstars and legends played like Ruth, Mantle, Yogi, Mattingly, Winfield and all those guys. So it was thrill for me to be able to play there."

Others come along feeling the same way.

"I was watching the World Series this fall and I saw Mark Grace going to Yankee Stadium for the first time in his life. And it was a thrill for him to b able to walk by all those monuments with Ruth, DiMaggio and those guys. To me, that I had the privilege to play over there and go over behind the wall and see all those great players is something that you will never forget. It's something that you will have in your heart all the time."

ROLLIE SHELDON

Well, The Truth Is . . .

Growing old is the worst crime a baseball player can commit. It's no wonder lanky pitcher Rollie Sheldon fibbed about his age when he broke in with the Yankees.

In 1961, Sheldon told the club he was 19 years old. He went on to post the best spring training of any rookie and won the James P. Dawson award as a result. However, before the team headed north it was discovered that Sheldon had actually served in the U.S. Air Force and attended some college.

His real age was 24.

The Yankees decided to keep the 6-foot-4 righthander, and Sheldon rewarded them with an 11-5 record and 3.60 earned run average during his initial campaign.

BUCK SHOWALTER

The First Day of School

B uck Showalter remains surprised at the opposition for his first regular season game as manager of the Yankees. "We beat the Red Sox, which I thought was pretty strange. With the troubles we were having drawing back then, I know it sounds crazy to say now, to play the Red Sox on Opening Day—a day you could play the Little Sisters of the Poor and fill the house up. I remember a pop up by Jody Reed to end the game. Steve Farr was pitching. I didn't think it would ever come down and thought it was foul. Charlie Hayes squeezed it, and I started thinking about my dad."

Buck Showalter's father, William Nathaniel II, died two weeks after he got the Yankee job. His son, William Nathaniel IV, was born a month later.

Get in the Car, We're Taking a Trip Downtown to Headquarters

Will any major league manager ever have a day more unusual than the one Buck Showalter had in 1992 when he was summoned before Commissioner Fay Vincent in the late morning before a day game?

"Fay Vincent called the house looking for me. My wife, Angela, told him it's a day game following a night game so he spends the night at the Stadium on a cot. So I get a call from the Commissioner's secretary shortly after my wife called to tell me what happened. I was told that 'the Commissioner had a problem with your testimony yesterday in the Steve Howe case and he would like to see you' at 11 or 12 o'clock sharp, I forget which. We had a game at one o'clock."

The Commissioner didn't care. Enter General Manager Gene Michael.

"He basically told Stick he was gonna be there for both of us and to worry about the game later. It was a pretty tough ride down there."

Then Showalter disappeared behind closed doors.

"I went in and told the truth. He had a problem with our testimony. He thought it contradicted the Commissioner's drug program. I can remember Fay Vincent smoking a cigar and having four or five of his people around him. The one thing I remember most was Jack Lawn."

Lawn was listed by the Yankees as Vice President, Chief of Operations.

"He was a pretty cool customer. He had been in the D.E.A. with the Bush Administration. I was the first one in and the first one out. He said, 'What happened?' I told him I was told that I had effectively resigned from baseball. Jack was reading a paper. He looked back down and said, 'Ah, he's bluffing, don't worry about it.' Jack went in and was told something like he should have checked his sense of ethics and morals at the door and done what's best for this Commissioner's Office."

That's when Jack Lawn pulled out a card and started writing.

"One of the security guys or henchmen or whatever, said to him, 'What are you doing?' He said, 'I just want to make sure I get that right. You've got to understand that I was in the Marines for 12 years. We were taught to never abandon our wounded and leave them on the battlefield. And that's the way we feel about Steve Howe.'"

The process left Showalter introspective.

"The question I had to ask myself was 'would I be down here on Steve's behalf if he had a 10.4 ERA and couldn't get anybody out?' The answer is yes and that is why I'm here. It was a pretty tough day. First-year manager. Stick was alright. Jack was cool as a cucumber. He had been through quite a few wars before. I just kind of followed their lead."

And then they returned to the park where many in the crowd did not know anything was amiss.

"I didn't get back until the third or fourth inning and we were behind 6-0 when we got back. I can remember putting on my uniform in my office. Stick was in there and I was thinking, 'the way this game is going, maybe I should just stay in here'. But I get out and I believe it goes, 6-1, 7-2, 7-3, 7-5, 8-5, 8-6, 8-7. I remember Pat Kelly got a basehit and we won the game 9-8."

Bleeding Pinstripe

Buck Showalter summarizes his time in the Yankee organization as follows:

"It was home, still is. It was an honor. I was a Yankee 19 years. I still consider myself a Yankee. It was where I was raised in baseball. There is a majority of my heart that will always be there."

Exiting Stage Right

In the wake of the Yankees' first playoff appearance in 14 years, suddenly, Buck Showalter was gone.

"I knew that under the circumstances Mr. Steinbrenner offered me the contract there was no way I could have done the job that needed to be done there with coaches that weren't mine. There wasn't anything else to it. If I could have kept my coaches, I would have stayed there until they ran me out of there. I left and didn't have a thing to stand on. I remember telling Angela, 'We may be in A-ball next year, who knows what's gonna happen. But I can't turn my back on these guys.' I couldn't watch him put coaches in that locker room that weren't mine. Everybody since then has been able to do that. I think he understands how important that is now."

Regrets?

Since Buck Showalter exited the organization, the Yankees came within three outs of winning four consecutive World Series.

"I don't think it's gut-wrenching to watch them. I think Joe realizes that there was quite a foundation that Gene Michael and a lot of people put together and he's kind of been a caretaker of it. I have a great deal of pride in what they've done. I know what it takes and what you have to do have championship clubs. To have all of that verified is very satisfying. I'm pulling for them. It's the first score I look for."

Buck Nostradamus

Know of anybody else in baseball history who helped craft the two teams that met each other in the World Series?

"Before the season started last year, ESPN asked all the baseball analysts to make predictions about divisional winners and go right on out. I picked Arizona and New York in the World Series with Arizona winning in seven games. They thought I was some kind of guru. But one guy said, 'Who else is he gonna pick?'"

Starting Small, I Mean, Real Small

I [Ed Randall] first interviewed Buck Showalter in 1986 when he managed the Oneonta Yankees of the New York-Penn League. He cherishes the experience.

"I was there in '85 and '86. Those years, I had spring training, ran extended spring in some place in the swamps of Florida. Then I went to Oneonta and then I headed right to the Instructional League. Angela and I went at it from February until November. You find out in a hurry if you want to do that for a living."

Even Then He Knew

Buck Showalter estimates that three-fourths of the players he had in extended spring training were first-year Latins.

"Bernie Williams, Hensley Meulens, Oscar Azocar, Deion Sanders was in extended spring."

Showalter had to talk Bernie Williams out of going home.

"He was so homesick. He wanted to quit switch-hitting. He was a 17-year-old kid who looked like Bambi drinking water out of a creek with the leaves rustling behind him. Beautiful man, though."

Just Back the Truck in on Payday, Won't Ya?

As Buck Showalter says, you find out in a hurry if you want to be in baseball.

"I was making twelve-five. I got a little stipend for the Instructional League. I went from $12,500 to $16,000 in '86. Then I got a three-year contract and thought I had the world by the coattails for 19, 25 and 32.

"Bobby Hoffman called me and asked me if I would consider signing a three-year deal. What else could you ask for, getting paid working for the Yankees and managing a baseball team?"

BILL SKOWRON

Pay Attention!

If Mariano Rivera completes a force play at second base in the bottom of the ninth inning of the seventh game, chances are the Yankees win the 2001 World Series. Likewise, if Willie McCovey's scorching line-drive with two outs in the bottom of the ninth of the seventh game, is two feet higher and not a bullet to Bobby Richardson, chances are the Giants and not the Yankees win the 1962 World Series.

For the Yankees, it's a damn good thing the ball wasn't hit to Bill Skowron at first base.

"Ralph Houk came out to the mound to talk to Ralph Terry. The Giants had second and third and they were discussing whether or not to pitch to McCovey or to walk him and face Orlando Cepeda with the bases loaded since McCovey's run meant nothing."

During this, Moose was getting sociable with first base umpire Jim Honochick, who later gained fame in the classic Miller Lite commercials.

"They're on the mound talking and I'm talking to Honochick. Houk's back in the dugout and I'm still talking to Honochick when McCovey hits the ball to Bobby Richardson. I couldn't believe it. It was the last out and the game was over."

Bill Skowron

Get this. Moose doesn't even think he was *looking* at the pitch that Terry threw.

"It was one funny feeling, I'll tell you that."

No Talking!

It's 1966 and Bill Skowron is a year away wrapping up his very substantial career and is playing for his hometown Chicago White Sox.

"Eddie Stanky is the manager. He didn't like the Yankees at all. We had a meeting prior to playing them and he says, "Anybody that gets caught talking to any Yankees, it's gonna cost you $50 bucks. So I'm on first base and Mickey gets a base hit."

Here, it's Mickey who wants to be sociable.

"I'm holding him on first and he says to me, 'How's the wife and kids doing?' I don't say anything. Again, 'How's the wife and kids?' Nothing. 'Moose, I'm talking to you.' I put my glove over my mouth and I say to him, 'I can't talk to you because it will cost me $50 bucks.' And Mickey says, 'All that money I made you in the World Series and I'm not worth $50 dollars?' I never thought he'd come up with something like that. He was a great man."

GEORGE STEINBRENNER

Sure-fire Bet

George Steinbrenner was an owner of the Florida Downs horse racing track, so it wasn't unusual for players to show up and plunk down a few bucks.

In 1978, Lou Piniella decided to plunk down some real money and invest in some racehorses during an auction at Hialeah near Miami.

Steinbrenner noticed Piniella and queried him as to what he was doing. Steinbrenner told him the horses at that particular auction were no good, so he led him to another private paddock where a sale was going on.

"This is where the good stuff is," Steinbrenner said.

Soon after the bidding began, Steinbrenner and Piniella agreed to go halves on a purchase. Piniella chose one filly, and received a nod of approval as the asking price soared to a final price of $43,000.

"We just stole one," a proud Steinbrenner confided. "We just stole one."

The filly's name was Proudly Dancing. Though the horse had never raced previously, Piniella shipped it to Monmouth Racetrack in New Jersey. A thunderstorm preceded Proudly Dancing's first race, but Piniella and the trainer decided to run her in the mud anyway.

George Steinbrenner

Proudly Dancer started last and finished last. Subsequent starts were also unproductive. Eventually she was sold for $7,500.

Whoops!

*   *   *   *

There's something about telephones that drove manager Billy Martin crazy. He hated the idea that owner George Steinbrenner called him during games or in the middle of the night.

After one such call, Martin ripped the phone right out of the wall in the clubhouse. When Steinbrenner queried a trainer as to why Martin's phone was out of order, he was informed why it happened. The Boss' reply: "Okay, tell him I'll call him tomorrow."

Another time Steinbrenner called the dugout and instructed Martin to fine catcher Thurman Munson for not wearing his baseball cap. One night at Chicago's Comiskey Park, third baseman Graig Nettles fielded a call from an irate Steinbrenner. Martin played it up as though an impersonator made the call and hung up, stunning Nettles. "Maybe he'll learn not to call down here anymore," Martin said.

*   *   *   *

Shortstop Gene Michael had a cold trick pulled on him one day in Texas.

A teammate shoved half of a hot dog into a finger hole on Michael's glove.

When the infielder ran out to his position and tried inserting his hand he was shocked at the discovery of something foreign, jumped up and threw his glove high in the air.

Compounding the joke was owner George Steinbrenner's reaction. He had a batboy fetch the wiener out of the glove and bring it to him. He was going to fine whoever put the hot dog wiener in the mitt in an incident which became known as The Great Wiener Caper.

CASEY STENGEL

The First Shot

It is often thought that Babe Ruth must have been the first player to hit a home run at Yankee Stadium in a World Series game.

In fact, it was Casey Stengel of the New York Giants who did it in 1923. In fact, Stengel homered in two games at Yankee Stadium, both Giants victories. While running the bases following the second homer, Stengel thumbed his nose at the Yankee bench.

Yankees owner Colonel Jacob Ruppert filed a complaint with baseball commissioner Kennesaw "Mountain" Landis, who denied the request for punishment. Babe Ruth was asked how he felt about Stengel getting away with his impish stunt.

"I don't mind," he said. "Casey's a lot of fun."

It's Crazy Over There

During his early playing days, Casey Stengel played for a minor league team in Maysville, Kentucky. Fittingly, an insane asylum was located just beyond the outfield fence.

Casey Stengel

The residents used to whoop and holler whenever Stengel left the field because he would practice his slide into third base before heading into the dugout.

How birdy was Stengel? In 1918, as a member of the Pittsburgh Pirates, the fans at Ebbets Field welcomed the former Brooklyn Dodger with a chorus of boos. With that, Stengel removed his baseball cap and a little sparrow flew out.

"The Old Perfesser"

The most famous nickname attached to Charles Dillon "Casey" Stengel was "the old Perfesser." He did not receive that moniker as field manager of the Yankees or Mets, two clubs he managed while he was in his 70s. In fact, he picked up that nickname in 1914, when he was 24 years old, during a spring training coaching stint with the University of Mississippi.

Say It Again, Casey

During one spring training in Arizona, Mickey Mantle was clubbing the ball as he never had before.

Naysayers said the thin desert air was the reason for it. Not so, Casey said, in his own form of "Stengelese."

"All I hear from you guys is talk about the stratmosphere," Stengel said, obviously referring to the atmosphere. "All I can say is the rest of these guys are hitting in the same air as this kid, and they ain't knockin' balls over the fences the way he is. Stratmosphere my eye! Mantle just hits hard, and you'll see that when we play in other places."

Second Show At 11

Casey Stengel was a master of one-liners.

"Anyone comes looking for me, tell 'em I'm being embalmed," he would say. Not long after being named the 1949 manager of the year, Stengel ran into the previous year's selection, Billy Meyer of the Pittsburgh Pirates.

"Ain't it funny, Bill, how all of a sudden I got so smart and you got so dumb?"

Tall Task

What kind of pressure was Casey Stengel dealing with as manager of the Yankees?

"The Yankees don't pay me to win every day—just two out of three."

Over 12 seasons, Stengel's Yankee teams won 1,149 games and won every American League pennant between 1949 and 1960, with the exception of 1954 and 1959. His teams also won seven World Series titles.

Accurate

Greg Goosen said the best thing Stengel ever said about him was the following.

"We got a kid here named Goosen, 20 years old, and in 10 years he's got a chance to be 30."

Really, He Said These

Some more Stengelese quotables:

• "Satchel Paige threw the ball as far from the bat and as close to the plate as possible."

• To Tommy Henrich: "I don't want you to sit in a draft. Don't slip and fall in the shower. And under no circumstances are you to eat fish, because them bones can be murder. Drive carefully, and stay in the slow lane, and sit quietly in the club-house until the game begins. I can't let anything happen to you."

• "They say some of my stars drink whiskey, but I have found that the ones who drink milkshakes don't win many games."

• "Right now we playin' bad every place. Not hittin', not pitchin' and not fieldin' too good. And judging by what I read in the newspapers, the Yankee writers are in a slump, too."

• "Left-handers have more enthusiasm for life. They sleep on the wrong side of the bed and their heads get more stagnant on that side."

• "If we had batting helmets when I was playing, John McGraw would have insisted that we go up to the plate and get hit on the head."

• "As great as the other men were on the ballclub, there comes a time when you get a weakness and it might be physical."

MEL STOTTLEMYRE

Mr. Grand Slam Himself

In 1965, Mel Stottlemyre won 20 games for a Yankee club that only won 77, pitched 18 complete games and led the league with 291 innings pitched. Oh, and hit a grand slam...inside the park.

"We were in New York playing Boston. I think it was in about the fifth inning. We were behind in the game and the pitcher was Bill Monboquette. I think the pitch was a hanging slider on the outside part of the plate. With me being a pitcher, Yastrzemski was playing shallow in left. The center-fielder was shading me toward right so there was this huge gap in left-center."

Stottlemyre hit a line-drive.

"It was just like a line-drive single but it was hit right in that gap and rolled forever out there in left-centerfield. I knew right away that it was extra bases, but I remember coming around third and was completely shocked when Frank Crosetti kept waving his arms in the coach's box for me to go on. It was such a long distance between third and home and everybody thought I made a great slide at home. To be honest with you, it was a fall."

Stottlemyre won the game 6-3.

Who Wants to Pitch?

The 1969 All-Star Game in Washington, D.C. was scheduled to be the first one ever played at night. Problem was it
poured and was played the next afternoon. Either time, Denny
McLain was tabbed to start for the American League.

Paging Mr. Denny McLain. Mr. Denny McLain to the white
courtesy telephone.

"It was a shocker to me that I was going to start. I didn't
know until I got to the ballpark. I'm on the bus and knew I had
a good chance to get an inning or two in. I didn't know up until
about 45 minutes before the game that I was starting. Denny
McLain just never showed up. It was a thrill even though I lost
the game. I would have preferred my start was under some other
circumstances at least knowing about it and that sort of thing."

Mel Stottlemyre hung a slider to Johnny Bench for a two-run
homer and was the losing pitcher as the American League was
defeated 9-3. Nobody ever did find Denny McLain.

A Cancer Survivor's Survivor

Since 2000, Mel Stottlemyre has defined courage in his fight
against a cancer that knows no cure, multiple myeloma. This,
after losing an 11-year-old son to leukemia.

"Myeloma was found through a regular team physical. I
didn't know what myeloma was and how serious it was. I
found out it was a disease of the blood. I was real concerned
and I guess was a little bit scared. But the more I found out
about the disease and the more reassuring things I got from
my doctor helped tremendously. I think my attitude changed
after I went to see the doctor at Sloan-Kettering. He painted a
much different picture than what I had been told by the doctors

previously in Florida. It was a tremendous shock. My disease, fortunately, was smoldering and I went 13 months before I had to start treatment. I think in a sense this probably was a little blessing for me. I knew I was gonna have to face the treatment but I had an opportunity to think about it ahead of time. I think my attitude changed a great deal. I became more optimistic about the treatments that were available through my doctor in New York at Sloan-Kettering."

In at least one other cancer survivor's eyes, Mel Stottlemyre has become a living, breathing testimony to those people who think that diagnosis is a death sentence.

"It isn't. I think we've come so far in recent years with the treatments and the things they can do for the disease. We can't talk about a cure but they are very optimistic about extending our lives. Naturally, I don't feel good about having the disease. But I feel real good that things have gone very positively for me and I've been able to paint a different picture than what we had before, that the word 'cancer' when it strikes us, everything has to completely change in our life. I don't think it does. Through the modern-day care that we have where things have gotten better, I think if we so chose we can continue the normal life we had before. Still in the back of our mind that word is always there and we have to learn to live with it. But it certainly isn't as drastic as it was as recently as just five or ten years back."

Perspective

One former cancer patient sees losses differently.

"I don't think I take the losses any lighter. I've always hated to lose or to accept losing unless you lose the right way. I feel real bad when one of my guys has a bad day."

But the sting is less.

"It certainly doesn't last as long. I look at things and think, 'Well, it's a loss but it's gonna pass quickly. We've got tomorrow to try and make it up.' So my attitude toward those things has changed greatly. I joke with some of the guys sometimes when they're so perturbed about some little thing that may be happening in baseball or it may be a thing that's happening in their life that's a very simple thing. It's not anything that's life-threatening or anything like that. And I really downplay those things. I say, 'That's nothing.' It's not life or death. It really has made me look at my entire life and people around me in a much different way.'"

Me too.

Stottlemyre vs. Stottlemyre

The only element missing from the electric 2001 World Series would have been for Mel Stottlemyre to have the opportunity to watch his son, Todd, pitch for Arizona against his Yankees.

"That would have been a huge thrill. I felt bad when we lost. I thought it was a great Series. As great a Series as it was for the Arizona Diamondbacks, it still was kind of tainted, I think, in Todd's mind because of the fact that he wasn't able to perform."

It's something the two Stottlemyres had long talked about.

"We've come close. We've had playoff games, we've had regular-season games where he's been on the other side. I tell you what, I'm sure whether I'm really up for it. I think the Series itself would have been even more emotional."

RON SWOBODA

Awed

Time had barely passed between Ron Swoboda's heroics in 1969 with the Mets and arriving as a Yankee in 1971. "I was gonna tell you this story anyway. I was not prepared to be awed. We had won a World Series with the Mets. It was not that long ago. In 1971, the second half of the season, I got traded from Montreal to the Yankees, which was like getting let out of limbo and back into the real world."

Swoboda remembers the first time he put on the pinstripes.

"I walked through the locker room into the hallway that led you into the home dugout and up those steps. And when I came up those steps all by myself wearing the Yankee pinstripes for the very first time, the first thing you see is the façade that used to be on the old Yankee Stadium and the monuments as you got on to ground level."

Thirty-one years later, the emotions still stir.

"I looked out there and as I'm telling you the story right now, I can feel the little hair on my neck start to stand up. It gave me a chill. It gives me a chill to this day to think about that very first time. I was not prepared to be awed. And I was awed. Everything came in a big rush. It was like me and Babe Ruth, two boys from Baltimore that played for the Yankees. And then the comparison starts breaking down."

And then Ron Swoboda started laughing. Swoboda and Ruth, two guys mentioned in the same breath to this day.

There's Playing in Yankee Stadium and Then There's Playing in Yankee Stadium

Before joining the Yankees, Ron Swoboda played in Yankee Stadium as a member of the Mets in a series of Mayor's Trophy games.

"No big deal. It was an old, dingy other-generation ballpark built in what, 1923?

"But I also played there as an amateur in the Hearst All-Star Game. The Hearst newspaper chain used to sponsor an all-star game with players from all around the United States. Then you'd play the New York all-stars. And I played in that game. I think it was 1961."

Swoboda's performance was, well, let him tell you.

"I was an abysmal failure. There was a pretty good player who played in the game for us named Tony Conigliaro. He starred in the game and might have been the MVP. He was good. I was scared to death. I was absolutely petrified. I didn't do anything, couldn't get the bat going."

Making an Immediate Impression

Ron Swoboda will never forget the start of George Steinbrenner's stewardship of the Yankees.

"We were in Milwaukee and Ralph Houk didn't know who George Steinbrenner was. I remember he got us all together in the locker room and he says, 'I'm gonna read off some numbers and these are the numbers of guys who need to get a haircut.'"

Swoboda is laughing.

"That was our first encounter with the sensibilities of George Steinbrenner in 1973 when he had taken over the team."

Houk must have loved that.

"There was nothing but sarcasm in Ralph's voice because it was kind of superseding his authority as the manager. It was guys like Bobby Murcer. But George didn't even know their names. You just sent the numbers in."

Swoboda is laughing again. But he stops when he talks about when Houk was let go.

"I remember the words: 'I've been retired.' And he was tearful. Everything he was as a ballplayer was with the Yankees."

FRANK TEPEDINO

The Events of 9/11

Frank Tepedino has served the City of New York as a firefighter after playing in the majors in 1967 and again from '69 to '75. His two sons followed and a brother are also in the FDNY.

"My one son is coming in from working a 24-hour tour but my brother is on vacation. I turn on the TV and I see the fire. He said, 'Did you hear about the plane that went into the Trade Center?' I said, 'Oh my God, you've got to be kidding me.' I remember being a little kid and reading about the plane that hit the Empire State Building in '46. I said, 'Not again.' It's kind of unusual for a small plane to be off course like that. When we were watching it, we found out a big jetliner went into it. But we still didn't believe that it was terrorism until the second one hit.

"I knew my other son was going in to work later that day. I had to make sure he was OK. We just jumped in a car and all headed in with two other guys we picked up on the way. We got in there as soon as we could. We had no problem getting in."

By this time, the World Trade Center was gone.

"It was just on such a massive scale, it was unreal. We were there for about 38 hours straight. I lost one kid from our firehouse. There had to be a good 50, 60 others, easy, that I knew by name and probably about 150 by sight.

"Emotionally, it was like a loss in the family but then it goes a little bit further. It's the camaraderie of the job. I've always said it's like being a part of a team. It's the loss that was so senseless."

Reaching out ... finally

In the fall of 2001, Frank Tepedino was selected by the Yankees to throw out the first ball prior to one of their Divisional Series playoff games against Oakland. He found it ironic.

"It was funny because I hadn't heard from the Yankees in 30 years. I thought somebody was just fooling around. There were so many reporters calling, so many news articles about the kid we had lost. When I got the call to throw out the first pitch, I was like, sure, OK. And then to get to the ballpark and to know that you're gonna part of something like that for the kid we had lost."

It was special to Tepedino because he felt like he was acting on someone else's behalf.

"The kid we had lost was such a big Yankee fan. We invited his mom and dad and his brothers and his sister to the game that night. Everyone knew the reason I was walking out to the mound to throw out the first pitch was because of this kid. It gave them a little bit of solace about losing their son. Here you are in the middle of America's pastime and his name was mentioned. The family really, really appreciated something like that. So it meant a lot."

BOB TEWKSBURY

Been There, Done That

Here's a question for you, Bob. Now that you're coaching Little League, is there anything you take from your days as a major leaguer and impart to the kids?

"Tom Kelly has a great phrase: to play the game. I remember when Mike Pagliarulo who was a teammate on the Yankees was on the World Series team with the Twins in '91. When I played with him in Texas in '95, that was his saying."

That was what the Twins have always done.

"They've always played the game. They have always been noticed for the way they hustle to first, the way they carry themselves on and off the field, the way they do these things and it's not coincidental."

Tewksbury imparts that lesson.

"What I try to say to these kids is we're gonna go out and we're gonna play the game. I don't care if we're gonna play the first-place team or the last-place team, I don't care what line-up I'm sending out there, if it's the best little leaguer or the not-so-talented little leaguer, but we're just to play the game and have fun."

Having seen the other side, Tewksbury enjoys his work but doesn't take it too seriously.

"I laugh at all the people who think that their kid is gonna be the next Ken Griffey Jr. and they have batting gloves and baseball camps year-round.

"And they're 10."

JOE TORRE

Heartfelt

Rocco Torre died of a heart condition while watching television as his brother, Joe, managed the Yankees. At the wake, Joe took the lineup card from that game and placed it in his brother's coffin along with a Yankee cap.

Frank Torre, a member of the 1957 and 1958 Milwaukee Braves World Series teams, was the next family member to have heart problems. While Joe was leading the Yankees to a pennant, Frank waited for a heart transplant. Frank got his new heart in the midst of the playoffs.

Finally, A Ring!

Joe Torre played 18 years and managed for 14 more with no World Series ring.

It wasn't until the Yankees finished off the Atlanta Braves in Game Six of the 1996 Fall Classic that his streak of 4,272 games without the ring would come to an end.

"I've never been so happy," Torre said after taking a celebratory victory lap around Yankee Stadium. "I never thought this would happen to me."

Joe Torre

His players thought it would.

"He kept saying, 'We will win this thing,'" reliever John Wetteland said. "Joe was the constant. No matter what happened, he never got too high or too low. He remained a rock for this team."

MIKE TORREZ

A Chili Reception

This is how Mike Torrez came from Oakland to the Yankees. "Charlie loved making chili. He was in the clubhouse and he had made some chili. He made pretty good chili. We were talking about him giving me the recipe. He wanted to sign me for a three-year contract at that time for $75,000, $125,000 and $150,000."

That's all beneath today's major league minimum salary.

"I said, 'Thanks for the three years but that's not enough money. You gotta come up with more money, that's nothing.' He said, 'Mike, if I can't sign you, I'm gonna try to trade you.' I said, 'That's fine.'"

Now the As are in Anaheim and Torrez is in the hotel lobby reading the paper. Joe Romo, the trainer at the time comes over and says he has a phone call. It's Charlie.

"I go over to the phone and he says, 'Doggone it, Mike, I'd love to keep you but it doesn't like I'm gonna be able to, so I made a deal. I traded you to the Yankees for some players.' I said, 'Well, alright' and went over to the stadium to get my stuff out of the locker. That's how the deal was made."

A Different Perspective on
B. Dent's Fly Ball

Here's the question: if Bucky Dent does not foul the ball off his foot and there's a stoppage in play, is history different?

"Probably. I was in a good groove. I was concentrating well. I had to get restarted again and on that first pitch, it was like 'goddamn it.'"

And then Torrez watched.

"Up until that point, the balls were not going anywhere. There was a little wind blowing in. For some reason, later in the afternoon, about the sixth inning, it changed and started blowing out. I was walking off the mound toward the dugout and looking up thinking I was out of the inning. I saw Yaz and thought that he had it. He looks up and sonofabitch..."

Tom Tresh

How Many Times Does it Happen That the Guy Who Makes the Great Catch Usually Leads Off

O r so it seems. In 1967, with the score tied 6-6 in the top of the ninth at the Stadium, Danny Cater of the White Sox, a future Yankee who was the swag for Sparky Lyle, hit a drive to deep left field.

"I dove into the stands and caught it and robbed him of a home run. It was really a neat thrill because when you make a great play, the fans are standing and cheering me and you run all the way back in with the third out into the dugout and the fans are still cheering. Well, I happened to be the leadoff hitter."

When Tresh stepped outside of the dugout, the fans started cheering again.

"It was a constant noise directed at you and what a thrill! I got up the plate and hit the ball out of the park to win it."

And the crowd kept cheering.

Checking the Outfield Defense, It's Tom Tresh in Left, Mickey Mantle in Center and Roger Maris in Right

Imagine being Tresh.

With the military claiming the playing services of Tony Kubek for most of the 1962 season, Tom Tresh played short-stop well enough for the Yankees to eventually be named the American League Rookie of the Year. Kubek returned later that season and Tresh moved to the outfield.

"Ralph Houk called me in the office in Minneapolis in late August or early September and said that Tony was back. "You played really well and we need both of you guys in the office. Tony and Bobby played a long time together. You've done a great job filling that position and if you want to stay at shortstop, that's fine."

But Houk said he had an idea.

"He said, 'I'd like to put together an outfield of Roger Maris, Mickey Mantle and Tom Tresh.' Of course, that had a little bit of a ring to it, especially when your idol is Mickey Mantle. Ralph said left field would not be a platoon position anymore. If you go out there and want to do that, it's your position. You don't have to try out for it, I'm not gonna take you out of it, it's yours. You've proved you can hit and done very well for us defensively. A shortstop has all the tools to play the outfield."

There was just one tiny problem.

"I think the last time I had been in the outfield was junior high school.

"But a shortstop's position where you have to go back on the ball a lot, you're in on all the throws, you're in on the longer relays, your arm has to be pretty good. So if you can play short-stop, you really have the tools probably to play the outfield. Left field at the Stadium was unique because it was a short left field line. A lot of balls would be hit down that line and would bounce off the fence or the wall and into fair territory. Because of my shortstop background, I had a lot of success throwing guys out at second base. Throwing from left field to second base was very much like going in the hole at shortstop and throwing to first base. Same technique instead of throwing the ball in the air, it went in one hop. I had good success at it."

ROBIN VENTURA

A No-Hitter Like No Other

I t was a sunny Sunday in Chicago on July 1, 1990, a getaway
game for the Yankees. Greg Hibbard opposed Andy
Hawkins. Robin Ventura batted second and played third
base. 2:34 later, Hawkins had pitched a no-hitter…and lost 4-0.

"I just remember it was a really cold day. It was one of those
things where he really shut us down the whole game. I came
up later in the game with the bases loaded and two outs and
I hit a ball pretty good into leftfield. It was really windy Jim
Leyritz was actually playing left. The ball spun him around a
little bit. I figured the way the wind was blowing, it wasn't
gonna be a hit. The reaction of the crowd meant something
had happened. I found out later the ball hit off his arm or
something."

The two-base error cleared the bases to give the White Sox
a 3-0 lead.

"It's just a weird thing to sit there on second base, a guy's got
a no-hitter and he's losing 3-0."

The outfield follies continued.

"Ivan Calderon actually hit a ball right after that and it was
also in the sun. Jesse Barfield got the ball but then dropped it for
an error and I scored. It's now 4-0 and the guy still hasn't given
up a hit. Just odd things you see in baseball."

Robin Ventura

O-Fer

After spending the 1989 season in Double-A, Robin Ventura skipped Triple-A and made the big club the following year. He started the season on fire, batting .350.

"You really start thinking it's easy."

It ain't. What followed was a slump of slumps of gargantuan proportions, 0-for-41. 16 straight games of nothing. .350 became .117.

"It was a long couple of weeks. For most of it, I didn't even make good contact. I just remember bad things happening."

Like a hit becoming an out.

"In Detroit, I hit a line-drive single to right. It one-hopped the rightfielder and he threw the guy out at second. It wasn't really bad baserunning. It was a hard play for the guy to read so it wasn't really his fault. When you're the hitter, you're thinking, 'Man, this is never gonna end.'"

The slump ended on a sacrifice that the pitcher overran. Ventura was given a hit.

Slammed

On May 20, 1999, playing as the Mets' 115th third baseman in their history against Milwaukee at Shea Stadium, Robin Ventura became the first player in major league history to hit grand slams in both games of a doubleheader. That gave him 15 career slams, the most among active players.

"The grand slams probably first came to my attention after about the eighth one. Once I hit those two in the doubleheader, I think people noticed me hitting grand slams a little bit more."

This good fortune depends on the pitcher.

"I've actually walked a few times with the bases loaded. Those are pitchers that aren't afraid to walk somebody in.

That's usually where the game comes down to with the pitcher where they don't want to walk a guy in for a run. They'd rather see if he could hit it."

Ventura says he doesn't get more fired up when he steps in with the bases loaded. He says it's just circumstances.

"Circumstances. You have to be lucky enough to get up that many times in that situation. I've also been fortunate to bat behind some good people that the pitcher obviously didn't want to face. So they took their chances with me and it kind of worked out for me."

The Yankees Then and Now

Times certainly have changed for the opposition coming into Yankee Stadium since Robin Ventura first came on the major league scene in 1990.

"Early on in my career, it wasn't like it is right now. You went in there expecting to win games and if you didn't come out of there with a couple, you were disappointed. Now, I think people go in there trying to get out with one and be on their way."

A Twist of Fate

It was just a routine spring training exhibition home game in Sarasota in 1997.

"It had been raining and they didn't know whether they should call the game or get it in. I was on second base and tried to score on a basehit. I slid into home and my spike got caught in the mud."

The injury was grotesque, shattering his right leg and ankle. Amazingly, Ventura said it didn't hurt. But it hurt to watch.

Omar Minaya, the new Expos GM, was a Texas Rangers executive in the stands that day. He compared its gruesome sight with that of Lawrence Taylor snapping Joe Theismann's leg.

"It felt weird. My body just went into shock. There wasn't really any popping or anything like that. That night, they explained the seriousness of it and what they had to do and how long it would take and the possibility I wouldn't play again."

Ventura spent four months on the disabled list during which time he had to learn how to walk again. There was even a question as to whether he would be left with a limp. There have been no problems since.

"I only go into the trainers room now for quality conversation."

FRANK VERDI

A Real-Life Moonlight Graham

Remember toward the end of "Field of Dreams" when Kevin Costner is sitting a room with Burt Lancaster, who's playing a former big leaguer named Moonlight Graham who never got a chance to hit? He laments that he wishes he had just had one at-bat.

This is the amazing story of 26-year-old rookie Frank Verdi of Brooklyn, New York in his eighth year of professional baseball.

"I'm in Boston and it's May 10, 1953. Back then, we left spring training before there was a final cutdown on May 15, so we had about 30 players. On his day, like any other, I took infield and batting practice and put my glove in the locker room never figuring I would get in the game."

"It must have been about the sixth inning and we're losing 3-1. Rizzuto was due to hit and Stengel said, 'Mize, you hit for Rizzuto.' So Mize pinch-hits. After the inning, he said, 'Verdi, you play short.' I almost fell over. I didn't have my glove there so I had to go running inside."

Verdi was now at shortstop for Rizzuto.

"Raschi was pitching and retired the Sox. In the next inning, we batted around. We had tied it up at 3-3 and had the bases loaded. I was in Rizzuto's lead-off spot. I remember Stengel yelling to me, 'Butcher boy, butcher boy.' That was one of his favorite expressions for chopping down at the ball. I think Ellis Kinder was pitching. He walked Raschi to force in a run and give the Yankees a 4-3 lead."

Verdi was next.

"I walk into the batter's box and the next thing I heard is 'Time out.' One of the coaches, Bill McKechnie, comes out to the mound and the next thing I know, they wave to the bullpen and change pitchers."

Verdi backs out of the batter's box.

"When the pitcher got through taking his warm-up pitches, I walked back into the batters box again. As I'm getting ready to hit, I hear, 'Time out' again. I said, 'What the hell is this now?' Stengel had called time out and I turned around and there was Bill Renna swinging three bats and loosening up. He came up to bat to pinch-hit for me."

Three days later, Frank Verdi was farmed out to Syracuse, never to return to the major leagues. He is listed, however, in the *Baseball Encyclopedia*.

You can't make this stuff up.

BOB WATSON

All Screwed Up

Bob Watson says, "It wasn't too much fun sometimes as the GM. It was another story when I played for the Yankees in 1980.

"We were at the Stadium playing Detroit in a double-header the final Saturday of the season. We won the first game and clinched the division pennant. So a lot of the regulars were given the second game off."

Manager Dick Howser started Bobby Brown in center. The switch-hitter was facing lefthander John Hiller.

"Hiller's best pitch was a change-up. Bobby Brown was a better hitter from the left side but he had to bat right-handed which he was not that good at but he was very strong on the right side. Brown leads off the game and I think Hiller jumps out in front of him like 1 and 2."

He throws him a change-up.

"Bobby starts his swing and sees that it is a change-up. He stops his swing but he stops it so hard and so abrupt that he hits himself in the head with the bat and goes down to his knees. Everybody in the dugout is just rolling. He looks over into the dugout and barely sees Howser and Yogi because everyone is laying on the floor in the dugout just laughing."

They say imitation is the sincerest form of flattery.

"For the remainder of the game, somebody says, 'Instant replay' and they would grab a bat, check their swing, hit themselves in the head and fall down to their knees. The game is over, we had just clinched the pennant and instead of a wild celebration, they were doing this Bobby Brown thing. It was one of the funniest things I remember seeing with the Yankees or anywhere else."

Setting the Record Straight

The popular notion in New York is that Bob Watson left as General Manager of the Yankees, the first African-American in baseball history to hold that position, to save his life, that working for George Steinbrenner was killing him.

"George Steinbrenner didn't help my health situation but he didn't cause it. I had it when I came. I had high blood pressure basically all my life. It runs in my family. What I did with the Yankees I did with Houston. I put in a lot of hours. I was trying to prove something not only to myself but to the baseball world that minorities have what it takes to run a ballclub. George had very little to do with me running myself into a health situation that I definitely had to leave. But he didn't cause it."

DAVID WELLS

Now it Can Be Told

Before deciding to play for the Yankees again in 2002, David Wells wanted to clear the air with once and future Manager Joe Torre.

"There were reports in the media saying that Joe really didn't care to have me back in New York," related Wells. "When I spoke with Joe, he said there was nothing to it."

Wells said if Joe didn't want him, why would he want to come back and play in New York for him? "It would just make things miserable."

Wells said he had a good conversation. "Joe said, 'The only reason why we traded you, it was Roger Clemens.' I understand that. Roger is a great pitcher."

"It's just something that happened. It was a business transaction. I could never understand why they would trade someone who wanted to be here and spent the rest of their life as a Yankee and all of a sudden, it's gone," said Wells.

"The only thing you could come up with is Roger Clemens and I can understand it. So Joe and I hashed it out and it was great."

David Wells

The Shirt off his Back and Back On It

Number 33 is back on the back of David Wells in a negotiation to be paid off later.

Yankees clubhouse manager Rob Cucuzza contacted last year's #33, Alfonso Soriano, upon the return of the Boomer. He gladly surrendered the uniform, never thinking to hold it hostage, though Wells offered a Rolex watch for its return.

"He had no problem giving up the number," said Wells. "That was a nice thing for him to do and I appreciate that."

Then Wells added, "It looks better on me. I have a wider back."

What Being a Yankee Means to Me

David Wells was always a rebel.

"I rooted for the Yankees as a kid because of the tradition. Everybody hated the Yankees when I was growing up. If someone hated something, I liked it," said Wells.

Wells remembers his Yankee introduction the first time.

"I walked right out to centerfield," remembered Wells, "and I got goosebumps like you wouldn't believe. Just having a dream come true playing in pinstripes was probably the best thing that every happened to me."

Now he is grateful for a return engineered solely by the Yankee owner.

"Most of all I want to thank George Steinbrenner very much for bringing me back." said Wells. "I think that was probably the best decision he's ever made and I thank him from the bottom of my heart."

Never In His Wildest Dreams

David Wells thought he would wear the Yankee pinstripes one day again.

"Yeah, as an Old Timer. You know how George likes to bring everybody back when you're 40, 50 years old and some," said Wells. "Coming back was never in my wildest dreams."

While on sabbatical from the Bronx, Wells had to get reaccustomed to going home after the regular season.

"In Toronto, the season would end around October 1 and I'd go up to my ranch in Michigan." It's the ranch he co-owns with former Tiger Kirk Gibson.

Wells got desperate.

"I'd go scouting around town looking for a Little League playoff game, to be honest with you," admitted Wells. "I was jonesing for a big game to pitch, even if it was with 10-year-olds. I'd blow it right by them."

Wells on Wells

"It was tough the last three years not being in the playoffs. That's something that I really strive for and look forward to.

"I'm not afraid to take that ball. I want to be the hero, I want to be the goat, it doesn't matter to me because I can still sleep at night knowing that I went out there and did my best.

"That's what you really play for, to get to the playoffs and eventually to the World Series.

"There's a lot of guys that get tight booties. I'm not the guy who gets that. I want the ball because I want to set the tone. You can't take the competitiveness out of me."

The Ink Spots

How important is family to David Wells?

He has a tattoo of his late mother, Eugenia Ann, on his chest and another tattoo of his son, Brandon, on his shoulder.

Chat Me Up

Time-honored tradition says leave the pitcher alone while a no-hitter is in progress. David Wells knows that, but he craved attention during his perfect game bid against the Twins.

Not one player bit for fear of tempting fate.

"I just wanted to talk so it would ease my mind a little bit," Wells said, "but no one would come near me."

Finally, fellow starting pitcher David Cone decided to break the tension by suggesting that Wells break out his knuckleball. While Wells appreciated the chat, he did not take Cone's advice. Reaching the dugout after the eighth inning, Cone told him, "You showed me nothing out there, you wimp."

In the final inning, Wells got Jon Shave to pop out, struck out Javier Valentin and then got Pat Meares to pop out to right-fielder Paul O'Neill.

"This is great!," Wells shouted as he was congratulated by catcher Jorge Posada and the rest of his jubilant team.

A Real Gem Of A Guy

To show his appreciation to his teammates for making a perfect game possible, David Wells purchased gold diamond rings for each of them. Each ring had "Perfect Game" engraved on the top with the linescore and date on the sides.

Mad Hatter

David Wells is a historian of baseball, particularly of home run legend Babe Ruth, with whom he shares certain portly physical attributes. Wells is such a fan of the Bambino that he actually purchased a hat worn by Ruth and wanted to use it as his own. He was dissuaded from doing so by the team.

BILL WHITE

The Call of the Home Run of Russell Earl Dent

W
e hear it every year, Bill White's play-by-play call of Bucky Dent's cataclysmic playoff home run in 1978. Listen closely and he sounds surprised as the ball disappears over the Green Monster.

"Well, you don't know. You can't be surprised by anything up there. The fence is short and if you get under the ball, it's a home run. So it wasn't a surprise. Rizzuto taught me how to sound surprised."

Sending a Message

When the Yankees cast the net for a new broadcaster, Michael Burke was on a mission. Bill White said the club president wanted the ballclub to reflect the community.

"Mike Burke said he wanted a black broadcaster. He said, 'We're in the Bronx. We've got a lot of Hispanic people here. We have a lot of black people here and I want these young kids to realize they can do this.' With Mike, I think it was a social statement to the minority people in New York. To me, it was a challenge."

Especially when a front office official named Howard Berk called him.

"Somebody sent him a letter and had cancelled their box seats. It didn't disturb me but surprised me that somebody who could afford to buy box seats and obviously should be well-to-do was disturbed simply because a black man was going to broadcast Yankee baseball."

Later on, White asked Berk what happened.

"The guy must have had some clout because he got the tickets back, which disturbed me. I thought that if he felt that way, they shouldn't have given him the tickets back. They should have sold them to somebody else. In fact, I would have bought them if I had known that he wanted them back."

Scooter Scoots

It was the ninth inning of a Yankees nighttime exhibition game in Fort Lauderdale when Phil Rizzuto asked Frank Messer if he could get him anything. Messer made the huge mistake of asking for coffee. With that, Rizzuto exited.

Bill White had left the park in the sixth inning to pick up his daughters at the airport.

"When I got back to the hotel, the game was in the 17th inning about one or two o'clock in the morning and I heard Frank Messer doing the ballgame."

The next morning, White is back at the park preparing for another game. In pops Rizzuto and says the following: "Hey, Frank, here's that cup of coffee you wanted."

With Rizzuto, no two days were ever the same because no one ever knew what would come out of that mouth.

"We could rip each other a little bit. He'd call me 'a National Leaguer' and I'd call him 'a little bunter'. We never had, in my opinion, a cross word with each other. We never, over the 18 years I worked with him, had any kind of animosity."

RONDELL WHITE

Rondell White grew up in rural Gray, Georgia, population 2,000, about 90 miles from Atlanta. It is hardly a sprawling metropolis.

"We had one red light. Now we've got three."

White was a vital cog in the Jones County High School team that won the state championship. White batted third, two spots behind leadoff hitter Willie Greene, who came to the majors with Cincinnati before drifting off to Baltimore, Toronto and the Cubs.

Floyd White, Rondell's father, is an avid baseball fan who was a faithful viewer of the old "Game of the Week" on NBC.

As a free agent last winter, the front-runners for White were Seattle, the Yankees and the Cubs, who hoped to retain his services.

"Once the Yankees were in it, there was no other place I was going to go."

That made dad smile.

The Fall Classic

The World Series was played despite World Wars I and II, Korea and Vietnam, a depression and countless other cataclysmic events in our history. All except 1994.

Rondell White

That was Rondell White's rookie season with Montreal. When the players walked out after the games of August 11, Felipe Alou's Expos had a 74-40 record, by far the best in the National League. They were six games better than Atlanta, eight games better than Cincinnati, which led the Central, and 16 games on top of Los Angeles in the West.

Ken Hill, already 16-5, was Montreal's ace. Right behind him was Pedro Martinez at 11-5, a pitcher whose best days lay ahead of him. The closer was John Wettleland, who, after play resumed the following April, was the Yankee closer.

The outfield featured Larry Walker, a .332 hitter who was to move on to Colorado, Moises Alou, who hit .339, and Marquis Grissom. No wonder White was the fourth outfielder.

When they packed away the bats and balls, the Yankees had a 70-43 record, best in the American League, 6 1/2 games ahead in the East over Baltimore, three games better than Central-leading Chicago and 18 1/2 games ahead of Texas which led the West with a 52-62 record. Really.

Starting August 12, the leagues were forced to cancel their games on a day-to-day basis. The strike marked the eighth work stoppage in 23 seasons and the fifth players strike in history.

On September 14, Acting Commissioner Bud Selig cancelled the remainder of the 1994 season including the Divisional Series, the League Championship Series and the World Series, the first time that happened in 90 years.

Ever So Close

Rondell White witnessed the magic firsthand.

After Tino Martinez' dramatic home run in the ninth inning of Game 3 of the 2001 World Series, Rondell White was in Yankee Stadium for Games 4 and 5.

He was there with Clifford Floyd of the Florida Marlins. Together, not so long ago, they had come through the fertile

Montreal farm system and were young stars in the Expos out-field.

In Game 4, White and Floyd saw Scott Brosius incredibly replicate Martinez' feat in the ninth and Derek Jeter's home run win it in the tenth.

Then, Alfonso Soriano won Game 5 with a single to right in the 12th inning. They may have been the three most dramatic World Series games ever played in succession.

"It was unbelievable, the fans talking baseball on every pitch," said White. "There's nothing else like it. It gave me goosebumps."

ROY WHITE

Not 6-4-3 But 48-21-6

O ne of the favorite trivia questions for Yankee-files to ask is, "What are the three numbers Roy White wore? See above.

"I wore 78 in one of the spring camps early in my career. When I made the club as a rookie in 1966, you didn't ask for a number. The clubhouse man, Pete Sheehy, was in charge of assigning them. He gave me 48."

Soon, White became a regular.

"I was sent out in '67 but returned in '68 and put on 48 again. I was getting in the line-up, playing regularly and having a good year. At the All-Star break, I went to Pete and asked him if I could change the number. I was established a little bit and didn't want such a high number. I looked at what was available and took 21. I wore that for the latter half of '68."

After the season was over, General Manager Lee MacPhail called White into the office.

"He said that next year they were changing my number and they wanted me to wear number six. I said fine."

After White began wearing number six, Pete Sheehy went over to him and let him in on a little secret.

"He told me that was Mickey Mantle's number his rookie season, which I never knew. I was pretty honored because all great Yankees had worn the low numbers."

Overcoming the Scourge

On the all-time Yankee list, Roy White is fifth in games played, seventh in at-bats, ninth in hits and tenth in runs scored. He's in the top-20 in doubles, homers and RBIs.

Not bad for a kid stricken with polio.

"My memories of it are pretty vague. My grandmother was working in a hospital as a nurse's aide or something and she told my mom to call an ambulance. Polio was really going around a lot then and that's what I was diagnosed with. An ambulance came out and took me to the hospital."

White remembers being there a long time, as long as a month or two, getting shots regularly and spinal taps.

"I remember when I came back to school, they put me back a grade. Everybody had passed me. But then the next year, they moved me back. I guess the fact that they caught it early and my grandmother got me to a hospital and they were giving me penicillin worked. I was never affected by paralysis. I was lucky."

DAVE WINFIELD

Bird-dropping

Every player gets fined in baseball's kangaroo courts—
sessions when everybody is liable for miniscule fines
for missing signs and making mistakes, on and off the
field—but how many players get fined by local magistrates for
something that happened on the field?

Ask Dave Winfield.

The Yankee outfielder was warming up his arm between
innings at Exhibition Stadium in Toronto, when the ball he
threw in the direction of a seagull actually hit the bird in the
throat and killed it. It took several pitches in the ensuing inning
before anyone figured out the bird was deceased.

Following the game, two plainsclothes officers arrested
Winfield and took him to the police station. The Yankees' team
plane was delayed a half hour waiting for Winfield to post $500
bond on a cruelty to animals charge.

While annoyed at the delay, Winfield's teammates were
quick to make light of the event.

"Hey, Dave, did you plead not "gull-ty?'" asked Graig Nettles.

Manager Billy Martin pondered the moment and sarcastically
told some sports writers: "Maybe when the Blue Jays come to New
York next week, we should hold a memorial service for the bird.
We can bury it back there by the monuments with the Babe."

Dave Winfield

The ribbing went on for weeks. Fans at opposing ballparks flapped their arms like wings whenever Winfield came to the plate.

They All Wanted Him

Dave Winfield possessed great athletic skills. It is no wonder that he was drafted by four professional teams in the American Basketball Association, National Basketball Association, National Football League and Major League Baseball.

Um, Nevermind

The World Series stage is what Dave Winfield wanted the most in his career.

It turned out to be his undoing.

During the 1981 Fall Classic with the Los Angeles Dodgers, Winfield managed just one hit in 22 at-bats.

The rest of his Yankee days were marked with doom as owner George Steinbrenner tabbed Winfield "Mr. May," an obvious contrast to Reggie Jackson's heroics as "Mr. October."

BUTCH WYNEGAR

What Was That?

There's always a danger in having pitches called from the dugout. The Yankees were mired in a seven-game losing streak late in the 1985 season when they locked horns with the Baltimore Orioles.

The game was tied at 2 in the seventh inning. Baltimore's Alan Wiggins was on first base and Rich Bordi was pitching to Lee Lacy. With a 2-0 count, catcher Butch Wynegar looked into the dugout for a sign and saw manager Billy Martin call for a pitchout. Bordi threw wide, but Wiggins never strayed off the bag. He walked Lacy on the next pitch and Cal Ripken Jr. knocked in the winning run.

Wynegar would learn later that Martin did, in fact, scratch his nose because it itched; he never called for a pitchout.

DON ZIMMER

How Much is That Little Doggie in the Window?

Don Zimmer came to the major leagues with the Brooklyn Dodgers and played with pitcher Billy Loes, who once claimed that he lost a groundball in the sun.

"We were in Cincinnati and it was very close to the All-Star break. Buzzy Bavasi, the general manager, was on the trip with us. I might be wrong in numbers, but Billy was something like 10-1 or 12-1 or something. It was getaway day and Billy was walking down 5th and Vine and went by this little pet shop. He saw this puppy he liked. He went in and asked how much. Well, he didn't have that kind of money on him. He wanted to take the dog with him, put him on a plane and take him back with us to Brooklyn. So he went to Buzzy and asked if he could lend him two or three hundred dollars. And Buzzy said, 'For what?' Billy said, 'I saw a little puppy I wanted to buy and take home.'

"Buzzy said, 'I ain't giving you two or three hundred dollars to pay for some puppy to take back on the plane.'"

Here, Billy Loes took a stance.

"He says, 'If you don't wanna give me money to buy the dog, then the heck with it, I'm not pitching anymore.' Somebody said to him that he had a chance of winning 20 games. He said,

'What's the difference, if you win 20 games, then they're gonna expect you to do it every year.'"

The Zimmer Fence Company

A check-swing off the bat of Chuck Knoblauch in the post-season at Yankee Stadium struck Don Zimmer in the head, injuring his ear and eliciting the now-famous line, "100,000 ears in the ballpark and he had to get mine." Immediately thereafter, fences were erected in front of both dugouts, but they were not identical. On the fence in front of the Yankee dugout was a tiny white sign that reads: Zimmer Fence Company.

Here's the founder.

"When that ball hit me I thought I was hurt. I was stunned but not exactly knocked unconscious. But I went down. And when I went down I put my hand up to the left side of my head which I where I suffered a serious injury years ago. That's the first thing that came to my mind. I was numb. As I put my hand up, my hand's full of blood. I say, 'Oh my God, now what?' I'm laying there and they finally got me up and I can't believe how much blood I have in my hand."

At that time, Zim really didn't know exactly where he was hit.

"I was half foggy. They picked me up and laid me down up in the clubhouse and the doctor walked in. The first thing he said was, 'You're not even gonna need stitches.' That was kind a relief because, evidently, I wasn't cut that bad. What had happened after I was up on that table for a while and the doctors were looking at me and so forth was that I realized where I was hit. The ball hit me kind of in my neck underneath the jaw bone. It then went up and nicked my ear, sort of like the way you nick yourself shaving and the bleeding doesn't stop.

"That's where all the blood was coming from. I was relieved that it didn't me in my skull where I had been hurt before."

Don Zimmer and Joe Torre

Enter The Boss.

"While I was in the trainers room and the trainers and doctors were looking at me, George Steinbrenner came in and said, 'Well, we're gonna have to do something out there to protect everyone more. We're gonna have to put up some kind of a fence or something.' That's where it started."

But that doesn't explain the lovely parting gifts, though.

"The next day, there was this box in my locker. I didn't know what it was. It was this old helmet. It looked like it had been in a war. I blamed Mel Stottlemyre, the prankster. I said, 'You do this, Mel?' He said, 'No.' Then I thought it was Jeter. I went out into the clubhouse and I said, 'You do this?' He said, 'No.' The only guy left I thought did this was Steinbrenner. I put the helmet on and he was in the clubhouse. I said, 'George, did you put this helmet on my chair?' He said, 'No I didn't put that helmet on your chair. You don't have guts enough to wear that in the dugout.' I never dreamt of ever wearing that helmet in the dugout until he said that."

That was good enough for Zim.

"I took the helmet and set it between Joe and I. We had to get up for the national anthem. When it was over, as the team took the field, I just let the helmet sit. When we came in off the field, I called Knoblauch over and said, 'Knobby, you have any objections about me wearing this helmet while you're hitting?' He said, 'No, I think it would be neat.' I wore the helmet for three pitches and that was it."

Somebody, though, took a picture and that picture remains in our mind's eye.

It's a Small World

One swing from Bucky Dent broke countless hearts in New England on October 2, 1978, including Don Zimmer's, the manager of the Red Sox that fateful day. Of course it would follow that Zimmer would come to the Yankees and wind up renting Dent's house in New Jersey.

"I was trying to find a nice place to live. At that time, most of the Yankee families lived over in Jersey. Well, I didn't even know where to start. I don't remember who said to me that Bucky Dent was trying to rent his house in Wyckoff. Somehow, my wife got a hold of somebody, I guess, another wife, and found Dent. That's how it happened. It was a very nice house."

The Bride Wore White. . . And Had Dust on Her Shoes

In 1951, Don Zimmer, playing for the Brooklyn Dodgers' farm club in Elmira, New York, got married at home plate.

"We had a general manager by the name of Spencer Harris. He had been with the Dodgers for years. He had been down in Fort Worth as a general manager before that. He heard Ed Roebuck, who was a pitcher, and I in clubhouse talking about getting married. And when he heard that, his eyes perked up. He said, 'Would the two of you be interested in getting married at home plate?'"

Presumably, Zimmer and Roebuck were not getting married to each other.

"He said he had a couple of weddings like that in Fort Worth. We both kind of shook our heads. We thought that would be kind of neat. But it turned out when Eddie went home, either his family or her family didn't like the idea of getting married at home plate. They thought they ought to get married in church. He wound up backing out. So my wife and I went on and got married at home plate." *That Night!*

"Eddie and Janice got married that afternoon. Roebuck, being a starting pitcher, got to go on a three-day honeymoon. I played that night."

15 minutes later.

Just "Zim"

Don Zimmer has been around the game of baseball for what seems like forever.

He's managed against the Yankees, for the Yankees (on an interim basis) and has served as the right-hand man for Yankee managers. His knowledge of the game is immense, matched only by his affability and humor.

One time while the Yankees were struggling and Zimmer was coaching third base, he had a couple runners thrown out at home plate. He walked back into the dugout and proclaimed, "Aw, hell, I'm just trying to take some of the pressure off Roy (Smalley)." Smalley was struggling at the plate.

Using His Head

Zimmer was hit in the head with a fastball while playing for the Dodgers, and doctors had to put a metal plate in his skull.

One day the radio in Graig Nettles' locker was drawing a lot of interference.

"It must be you, Zim," Nettles said. "The plate in your head is messing up my radio!"

YANKEE MISCELLANEOUS

What A Playoff!

The three-ring circus that was George Steinbrenner, Billy Martin and Reggie Jackson kept the Yankees on the back pages of the New York tabloids during the summer of 1978 but not at the top of the American League East standings.

The Boston Red Sox held a comfortable lead, and tensions were getting hot in the Yankee clubhouse. Jackson had been suspended by Martin for five games for failing to follow signals. Martin felt he wasn't being backed up by Steinbrenner, and eventually snapped, throwing out the famous line, "One's a born liar and the other is convicted."

Martin's farewell came before television cameras in a Kansas City hotel on July 25.

In stepped mild-mannered Bob Lemon to take over the job. Two weeks into the job, on August 19, the Yankees still trailed the Red Sox by nine games. A solid run reduced the gap to four just as the Yankees visited Beantown for a four-game series. The Yankees ripped through the Red Sox, scoring 42 runs on 67 hits. New York moved into a tie for first place, having erased a 14-game deficit in just 53 games.

Inside a week, the Yankees had taken a 3 1/2 game lead but the Red Sox wouldn't quit. Boston closed the season with seven consecutive wins, the last a 5-0 shutout of Toronto. Meanwhile, Catfish Hunter failed to nail down the clincher against Cleveland as the Indians prevailed, 9-2.

Both teams finished at 99-63. The season would be extended by one more game, a playoff to be played at Boston's Fenway Park.

"If we lose we can blame it on George (Steinbrenner) since he lost the coin toss," third baseman Graig Nettles said of the playoff site determination.

A splendid fall afternoon greeted two teams who were as loose as they come, odd considering what was at stake. Yankees starter Ron Guidry (already 24-3 at that point) served up a second-inning home run to Carl Yastrzemski and a sixth-inning RBI single to Jim Rice. Meanwhile, Mike Torrez carried a shut-out into the seventh inning.

Chris Chambliss and Roy White reached on singles, but Jim Spencer flew out for the second out of the inning. Up stepped light-hitting shortstop Bucky Dent, who had just four home runs and was hitting an anemic .140 over the previous 20 games. Dent stood in and promptly fouled the second pitch off his foot.

As trainer Gene Monahan tended to Dent, Mickey Rivers handed Dent another bat. "Here, use this. I feel it will be lucky for you," Rivers said.

He wasn't kidding. Torrez hung a slider and Dent lofted a fly ball to left field that just wouldn't come down as it lazily carried over the famed Green Monster in left field for a three-run home run. "Bucky Dent had turned Fenway Park into the world's largest morgue," said Lou Piniella.

Thurman Munson kept the rally alive with a RBI double to knock in Rivers, who had walked and stolen second. Reggie Jackson homered an inning later to give New York a 5-2 lead heading into the bottom half of the eighth.

Jerry Remy doubled off closer Goose Gossage, and Yastrzemski singled him home. Carlton Fisk singled and Fred Lynn followed suit, cutting the lead to one. Gossage got out of the rally by fanning slugger George Scott.

A blinding sun gave Piniella fits in right field. With three outs to go, Dwight Evans popped out and Rick Burleson walked. Up stepped Remy, who hit a sinking liner to right. Piniella lost sight of the ball, but ran to where he thought it was going. Sure enough, he saw it just in time to lunge and corral the bouncing ball. He threw a lined shot to third baseman Nettles, holding Burleson, representing the tying run, at second base.

"Was that me or God who threw that ball?" Piniella pondered later.

Piniella made a catch on Jim Rice's fly ball to right-center but could not prevent Burleson from moving up to third base on the sacrifice. Up stepped Boston hero Carl Yastrzemski.

Nettles had seen Yaz power the Red Sox to the 1967 A.L. pennant over his own Minnesota Twins, and he prayed it wouldn't happen again.

"How about a pop-up right now?" Nettles said to himself, before changing his tune. "Not to me. Please, not to me."

Meanwhile, Gossage had no question as to what he was going to throw. "I wasn't going to mess around with any breaking junk," he said. "I wasn't going to get beaten by anything but my best. Yastrzemski's the greatest player I ever played against. I just wound up and threw it as hard as I could. I couldn't tell you where."

Yaz swung at Gossage's first delivery, a high fastball, and fouled it off in the direction of Nettles, who made the catch to wrap up the division title.

Piniella was grateful to God for having the opportunity to be on the field that day.

"I was excited for the moment, for myself, my family and my teammates. Most of all, I was excited for the organization. We understood the Yankee tradition that day. Even if none of us was a Ruth or a Gehrig or a DiMaggio or a Mantle, we had each carved our own niche in Yankee history, and that was something to be very proud of."

The Yankees not only beat the Kansas City Royals for the third year in a row in the A.L. Championship Series, but also beat the Los Angeles Dodgers in the World Series for the second consecutive season.

FIGHTIN' WORDS

Gonna Fly Now

Not all the fighting was left to the players. Following Game 5 of the 1981 World Series, owner George Steinbrenner got involved with two fans in a hotel elevator.

"I clocked them," Steinbrenner said proudly, even with his hand bandaged.

"There are two guys in this town looking for their teeth."

On the flight back to New York the next day, Lou Piniella passed by Steinbrenner and asked, "How are you doing, Rocky?"

That prompted a huge grin from the owner.

Catchers In The Fray

The Yankees' pennant drive of 1974 was waylaid by a brawl between catchers Bill Sudakis and Rick Dempsey.

Neither backstop was seeing much action behind Thurman Munson. Sudakis decided he would razz Dempsey about it as the Yankee bus made its way to a Milwaukee hotel.

Once there, Dempsey and Sudakis tried to go through the hotel's revolving door at the same time and the door jammed.

Once freed, Dempsey threw a punch at Sudakis. Sudakis lunged at Dempsey and the pair rolled over a table and onto a couch.

Bobby Murcer jumped into the fray to play peacemaker, and ended up hurting his hand. He was put out of the lineup and the Yanks lost the pennant by a game.

Still Old Foes

Sometimes old foes become new teammates, but remain foes. Case in point: Cliff Johnson and Goose Gossage. Early in the 1979 season, Johnson was steamed about being left out of the lineup one day. Johnson was asked how he had fared against the fire-balling Gossage in previous seasons, but before he could answer, Goose said, "He couldn't hit what he couldn't see," and laughed his way into the clubhouse sauna.

When the pitcher came out again, Johnson confronted Gossage and a huge rolling fight took place. The result was Gossage hurting his right thumb and missing action for the next three months.

Fam-uh-lee?

The Pittsburgh Pirates rode the theme, "We are Family," on the way to their 1979 World Series championship. Two years later, Yankee teammates were at each other's throats before the first pitch of the Fall Classic was thrown out.

The Yankees swept the Oakland A's—managed that strike year by none other than Billy Martin—and decided to celebrate their American League pennant at a Bay area restaurant. As the story goes, Graig Nettles' wife, Ginger, left her purse on her chair as she went to get something to eat. When she got back, the purse was missing and one of Reggie Jackson's guests was sitting in the chair.

An argument ensued, and Graig knocked Reggie down with two punches.

Put Up Your Dukes, Let's Get Down To It!

There's no Yankee fighting legend as good as Battling Billy Martin.

He fought with teammates, opponents, his own players, bar patrons and a marshmallow salesman.

Phil Rizzuto was quoted as saying, "Billy is like a gunfighter in those westerns. There is always some young guy who wants to take him on and prove something and Billy can't back away."

A 1985 trip to Baltimore produced back-to-back brawls for Billy. On the first night, an angry bridegroom accused Martin of insulting his newlywed wife, an argument ensued and the pair had to be separated by Yankee players and bartenders.

The next evening, disgruntled pitcher Ed Whitson and Martin went at it after the manager decided not to use Whitson for a start. What started as an argument between Whitson and another bar patron turned into an all-out punching and kicking brawl between Martin and Whitson. The pitcher ended up breaking Martin's right arm with a kick. Incredibly, neither Whitson nor Martin received any punishment from Steinbrenner.

At season's end, Martin demanded a raise of salary to $500,000, or he might not return. Not amused, Steinbrenner hit the right chord when he surmised, "Well, let's see. That'll be $200,000 for managing the team and $300,000 for being the first challenger to (heavyweight boxing champion) Michael Spinks."

Pitching A Fit

Sometimes a fight isn't actually a fight. In a May 1969 game between the Washington Senators and New York Yankees, Bobby Murcer homered off Senator Marty Pattin.

The next time up Pattin sailed a pitch over Murcer's head. Murcer eventually reached base and came in high with his spikes on a slide into Ray Oyler, prompting a bench-clearing brawl.

While Murcer and Oyler apologized to one an other while at the bottom of the pile, ex-Yankee Jim Bouton decided to pair up on the outside of the fray with Fritz Peterson. The old friends decided to put on a little show.

"How's your wife?" Bouton asked. "Give me a fake punch to the ribs."

"She's fine," Peterson replied. "You can punch me in the stomach. Not too hard."

Eventually, Peterson forced Bouton to the ground and the pair rolled around for effect, prompting two umpires to rush over to tell them to knock it off.

"But we're only kidding," Bouton said. "We're old roommates."

The umpire told them to break it up anyway.

Stupid Ballplayer Tricks

The heat of battle will force players to do many stupid things. On July 26, 1922, first baseman Wally Pipp misplayed a ball at first base, just another defensive lapse that outfielder Babe Ruth had been riding Pipp about for weeks.

Pipp was convinced Ruth would say something at the close of the inning, and sure enough Ruth did.

"For God's sake, Pipp," Ruth said, only to be hit in the face several times by the quick-swinging Pipp.

Having been pulled apart, Ruth told Pipp this incident would be settled after the game.

As it turns out, 15 runs would be scored in the final three innings. The Yankees beat the St. Louis Browns, 11-6, with the help of two home runs by Ruth.

Following the game a joyous Ruth bounded into the clubhouse only to be met by Pipp.

"I'm ready," Pipp said.

Ruth had forgotten his vow made in haste earlier and then waved Pipp away.

"Oh, Christ, forget it."

Howdy, Y'all

Not all of Ruth's fights took place at the ballpark. The Yankees conducted spring training in 1921 at Shreveport, Louisiana.

Sometimes, Ruth and some teammates headed into the countryside to find a roadhouse bar. One night the partying got too loud and a local man took exception.

An argument ensued, but peace was restored. The agitator left in a huff, as did Ruth later on in the Essex the city had given him for use during camp.

Pitcher Harry Harper noticed that a car left right after Ruth's did and he suspected there would be trouble. Harper and some teammates got into Harper's car and drove off to follow. They found Ruth's car on the side of the road and Ruth holding his hands up while the same man from the bar was pointing a gun at him.

Harper drove his car right at the man, who jumped to the side and was grabbed by Ruth.

Harper, who later would become the sheriff of Bergen County, New Jersey, disarmed the man and sent him away.

*　　*　　*　　*

Catcher Bill Dickey once was suspended 30 games for breaking a Washington player's jaw.

He did it with one punch during a dispute at home plate.

YANKEE STADIUM

The House

Yankee Stadium was built in less than nine months at a cost of $2.5 million. Ground was broken on May 5, 1922, as the Yankees played their 10th and final season at the Polo Grounds in upper Manhattan.

Not only did "The Yankee Stadium" (as it was originally known) have the largest capacity of any park of its time, it was the first to use the word "stadium."

The new ballpark opened on April 18, 1923, with a crowd of approximately 60,000 people braving the chilly weather (although the original announced crowd was 74,217, far beyond capacity).

New York Governor Al Smith threw out the first pitch and Babe Ruth was presented with a bat in a glass case.

The home plate umpire was none other than Tommy Connolly, who had called the first New York Highlanders game in 1903.

It was only fitting that Ruth hit the first home run in Yankee Stadium history, a third-inning three-run poke into the right-field bleacher seats off Howard Ehmke.

Before the game, Ruth had said, "I cried when they took me out of the Polo Grounds. Boy, how I used to sock 'em in there.

I'd give a year of my life if I can hit a home run in the first game in this new park."

Way Out There, And Still In Here

The first season at Yankee Stadium saw 20 inside-the-park home runs, an astounding figure unless one considers the field's dimensions.

While the lines were short (296 feet in right, 301 in left), center field was nicknamed "Death Valley" for its 461-foot depth.

Dandy Location

The site for Yankee Stadium, at the mouth of Crowell's Creek, was selected by owner Colonel Jacob Ruppert.

Having been kicked out of the Polo Grounds by the New York Giants tenants, Ruppert wanted to build a facility within sight of the Polo Grounds. It just so happened to be the same place baseball was born in the Bronx with the 1866 advent of The Unions of Morrisania team.

They Can See Clearly Now

The remodeled Yankee Stadium opened to over 52,000 fans on April 15, 1976.

Although there were more than 11,000 fewer seats, all the seats in the new ballpark were unobstructed.

Brand-spanking new, the ballpark wasn't received glowingly by veterans.

"They changed a lot of it," Fred Stanley said. "There were some things about it that were the same, but it wasn't the old Yankee Stadium."

Radio Days (And Nights)

America grew up listening to World Series game on the radio, including games being played at Yankee Stadium.

As a result, the facility became a destination point for world travelers.

"When I was a kid," said right-handed reliever Pedro Ramos, "I used to listen in Cuba on the radio to the World Series and hear names like Yogi Berra and Joe DiMaggio. I got them in my head. I knew that Yankee Stadium was history and like somebody wants to see the Grand Canyon or one of the wonders of the world, to me Yankee Stadium was and is the wonder of the baseball world."

Adds infielder Phil Linz: "It is the most magic baseball park ever built. Playing there as a Yankee was like being in the Marines, the feeling that you were in a special ballpark, special town, special uniform, special history."

"Just walking into Yankee Stadium chills run through you," said pitcher Jim "Catfish" Hunter.

Bronx Battlers

Five Yankees were waiting for some last-minute woman chasing before a midnight curfew one night in St. Louis, where Billy Martin caught the ears of five women coming out of the lobby of the Chase Hotel.

However, five male friends also came out and were upset with the players' advances. A fight was about to ensue when Ralph Houk and Hank Bauer started to argue over who was going to start the brawl. It was decided Houk would, since any injury to him wouldn't hurt the club as much.

Houk proved to be a tough fighter. He knocked down one of the men three times, with a distraught Mickey Mantle going over each time to pick the man up and wipe blood from his face with a handkerchief.

Finally, the beaten man grabbed Mantle's arm and said, "Buddy, I don't know who the hell you are, but would you mind staying out of this fight?"

*   *   *   *

Ralph Houk was also at the center of a bar brawl, also in St. Louis, that nearly turned ugly.

A female bartender took exception to comments made by one of the Yankee ballplayers, and soon a handful of bar bouncers showed up. One of them pulled a gun, and Houk reacted by breaking a bottle and holding the jagged edge to the man's throat. All together, the Yankee players backed out of the bar and hopped a cab out of trouble.

CHARACTERS, GOOD AND BAD

No Neck Williams

With his thick, fire-hydrant build and seemingly non-existent neck, Walt "No Neck" Williams became one of the game's most recognizable figures of the sixties and seventies. A cult figure and fan favorite with the Chicago White Sox, the five-foot, six-inch Williams always had a smile and seemed genuinely thrilled to be playing games in the major leagues. White Sox fans loved his upbeat attitude and his willingness to hustle. Not surprisingly, more than a few Sox diehards reacted with anger in October of 1972, when they learned that the White Sox had traded No Neck to the Cleveland Indians for middle infielder Eddie Leon.

Williams batted .289 in his one year with the Tribe, but the Indians made him part of the bait in a three-team spring training trade that fit No Neck for the pinstripes of New York. While with the Yankees, Williams firmed up his reputation as one of the more interesting characters in the game. Both before and after each game, Williams completely slathered his body, head to toe, in Vaseline. He apparently believed that the slippery substance was good for the skin, but it must have created a few awkward moments during pre-game handshakes.

Williams also displayed a voracious appetite, regularly accompanying Yankee first baseman-DH Ron Blomberg and shortstop Gene "Stick" Michael on trips to local Burger King restaurants, where they happily consumed large quantities of hamburgers at 39 cents a pop. (During one memorable sit-down, Blomberg finished off 28 hamburgers!) The burgers complemented No-Neck's stocky 185-pound frame.

Williams' legendary appetite stood out as one of the highlights of his term in New York, which coincided with the two seasons the Yankees played at Shea Stadium. In his two summers with the Yankees, Williams filled in as a backup outfielder and made some cameo appearances at second base. He did hit fairly well in a bench role in 1975, batting .281 as a utility outfielder and backup second baseman, but the Yankees released him prior to the 1976 season. Unfortunately, that denied him an opportunity to play in his first postseason, as the Yankees advanced to their first World Series since 1964.

With his major league career over, there were no playoffs or World Series for Walt Williams. He just had to settle for ten big league seasons in which he made plenty of friends with teammates and fans. And he'll always be remembered for being No Neck.

Mel Hall

As the Yankee organization mucked through a difficult decline in the early 1990s, Mel Hall was one of the few bright spots. He brought clutch hitting, hustle, and some much-needed color to the pinstripes. Although Hall had his limitations—he never walked much and couldn't throw worth a damn—he hammered right-handed pitching and ran the bases hard, even drawing praise from Don Mattingly for his constant effort. Hall could also provide some carnival sideshow entertainment.

One of the game free-spirited characters, Hall called his fielding glove "Lucille." He liked to wear batting gloves in his back pockets as a way of waving "bye-bye" to opposing pitchers after home runs. He also stunned a conservative New York organization by once bringing his two pet cougars into the Yankee Stadium clubhouse. Members of the Yankee front office, along with some of his teammates, were not exactly thrilled by the visit from two wild animals. Hall, who lived in Trump Towers, regularly walked his cougars on the streets of New York City. In 1990, the city confiscated the cougars and fined Hall $10,000.

The incidents with the cougars could have been interpreted in two different ways. On the one hand, Hall was clearly breaking the law and putting innocent people in potential danger, especially if he ever lost control of his "pets." And yet there was something amusing, like a skit out of an old "Benny Hill" episode, about a man bringing a couple of cougars into the hallowed halls of Yankee Stadium.

Unfortunately, some of Hall's other stunts were less open to interpretation. Hall took a wrong turn when his initial rookie "hazing" of a young Bernie Williams evolved into mean-spirited tormenting of a sensitive teammate. Hall needled Williams so mercilessly that he practically drove the future star to tears. Even the veterans on the Yankees felt that Hall had gone too far. That sentiment came to be shared by the team's front office, which allowed him to leave as a free agent despite a productive 1992 season.

Hall's escapades with hazing and cougars seem trivial in comparison with later problems. After his playing days, Hall fell off the moral track completely when he engaged in a reprehensible sexual relationship with a 12-year-old girl. Convicted on three counts of aggravated sexual assault in 2009, Hall received a sentence of 45 years, with eligibility for parole in 22 years. In other words, the sentence will keep Hall in prison until he is at least 70, and possibly until he is 93.

At one time, when there wasn't much else to root for, Yankee fans enjoyed watching Mel Hall deliver clutch hits against the Boston Red Sox. Now they probably just wish that he never played for their team at all.

THE CHAMPIONSHIP
SEASON OF 2009

Jeter Joins Gehrig

Publicly, Derek Jeter has never expressed much interest in personal goals and achievements. So it was only appropriate that in the same season he set a notable franchise record, his Yankees ended up winning the World Series. Winning, after all, trumps individual statistics.

Still, Jeter's achievement became an important part of Yankee lore. Breaking any Yankee record that was held by the legendary Lou Gehrig must be considered a major accomplishment. No player had collected more hits as a Yankee than Gehrig, the game's respected and revered "Iron Horse."

On September 11, 2009, Jeter and the Yankees hosted the Baltimore Orioles at the new Yankee Stadium. Jeter entered the Friday night game with 2,721 hits, the same total accrued by Gehrig before the effects of ALS forced him from the Yankee lineup in 1939. In the third inning, Jeter stepped in against Orioles right-hander Chris Tillman. He promptly laced one of Tillman's offerings toward the right side of the infield. Baltimore first baseman Luke Scott dove for the ball but missed, the line drive bounding safely on the outfield grass. Fittingly, with his trademark opposite-field stroke, Jeter had collected hit No. 2,722, surpassing the mark of the beloved Gehrig.

As Jeter touched up at first base, his teammates streamed from the Yankee dugout onto the infield to congratulate him, stopping the game. Jeter likely felt uncomfortable with his teammates' gesture, but it was certainly an appropriate reaction to a record set by a man who had been exclusively a Yankee since his debut in 1995, helping the franchise to four world championships along the way, with a fifth title in the offing.

The record-setting hit came with an extra degree of anticipation, given the heavy Bronx rains that delayed the start of the game by an hour and a half. Jeter's hit came amidst a steady rainfall, which continued throughout the evening. Not wanting to miss out on witnessing history, most of the 46,771 fans attending the game had decided to wait out the delay amidst 25-mile an hour winds, and then spent a good portion of the game chanting Jeter's name.

Jeter added to his hit total one inning later, delivering another single to cap off a 2-for-4 performance. By the end of the day, Jeter's season average had risen to .331.

If there was a down side to the night, it was that the Yankees lost to the Orioles, 10-4. That fact could not have pleased Jeter. But six weeks later, that defeat to the Orioles would mean little to Jeter and the Yankees.

The Genius of Girardi

Throughout the historic season of 2009, Joe Girardi became a lightning rod for debate on Internet web sites and newspaper forums. Even in the midst of a 103-win season, Girardi still had his share of critics. Some said he bunted too much, brought too much tension to the dugout, did not tell the truth about injuries, and mishandled the bullpen, among other shortcomings.

Such is life in the age of the Internet and talk radio. Every manager, no matter how successful, is severely criticized by a percentage of his team's fan base. If you believe some fans, every manager makes out a bad lineup card. Every manager fails at handling the bullpen, an inevitable gripe when a manager has six or seven fulltime relievers. If you listen to the criticism long enough, you'll soon believe that every manager is the reincarnation of the village idiot.

Managers can never satisfy all of their constituents, but they can make a difference through their intelligence, their common sense, and their ability to relate to their players. These were all managerial attributes displayed by Girardi in 2009. He had shown similar tendencies during his playing days, as he managed to last 15 major league seasons, largely because of his keen handling of pitchers and his strong defensive skills.

Girardi showed few weaknesses in 2009. His biggest demerit might have been an overreliance on the sacrifice bunt. If that is anybody's worst offense as a manager, then that's an indication that the manager has done a good job. All in all, Girardi did quietly good work in 2009, leading the Yankees to the best record in baseball (103-59), in addition to impressive postseason performances against the Minnesota Twins, Los Angeles Angels, and the powerhouse Philadelphia Phillies. At the beginning of the season, the Yankees looked like no more than a 95-win team. After all, they had to endure the absence of Alex Rodriguez, who missed the first six weeks with a bad hip, forcing them to make do with a less-than-stellar replacement in Cody Ransom. A tough schedule and a difficult division also foreshadowed a rough summer. Yet, Girardi guided the Yankees to more than 100 wins, not to mention the 11 additional victories in the postseason. If anything, the Yankees overachieved, making Girardi worthy of praise, not criticism.

Girardi succeeded in relaxing the atmosphere in 2009, compared to the general tension he seemed to create in 2008. He made no glaring mistakes with his lineup, used his improved bench sufficiently, and distributed the workload in the bullpen evenly so as not to blow out any of his relievers' arms. Just as significantly, in terms of preparation and reviewing scouting reports, it would be difficult to find a manager who put in more hours or worked any harder than Girardi.

Yankee players were among those who sung the praises of Girardi. After the Yankees clinched the American League East on a Sunday afternoon, reporters asked Rodriguez who should be considered the team's MVP. Rodriguez listed the accomplishments of several teammates, but then ultimately answered "Girardi." And when the results of the AL Manager of the Year award were announced, no one should have been surprised when Girardi received four first-place votes and finished third in the balloting, behind only the Angels' Mike Scioscia and Minnesota's Ron Gardenhire.

Joe Girardi, with his smarts, toughness, and willingness to work, showed himself to be a keeper during the championship season of 2009.

TRIBUTES

The Major

It is a fault of human nature, but it sometimes takes death to resurrect the memories of retired players and managers. Such is the case with Ralph Houk, who won two world championships while managing the Yankees, but became a forgotten man a few years after George Steinbrenner purchased the team. He then faded further into obscurity with the success of Joe Torre in the late 1990s and early 2000s.

The underrated Houk, who died in July of 2010 at the age of 90, deserves credit for being a patient, players-first manager who worked well in developing young prospects. With a little more luck, his legacy might have carried more powerfully into later generations of baseball fans.

Based on Houk's first three years as a manager, it appeared that he was destined for a place in the Hall of Fame. Succeeding the legendary Casey Stengel, he led the Yankees to world championships in his first two seasons, before falling short of a third consecutive title in the 1963 World Series against the Los Angeles Dodgers. If Houk had guided just one other team to a world championship, we might be celebrating him today as a resident of Cooperstown. But that third title became elusive. In fact, Houk never again finished first in the regular season—either in the Eastern Division or the American League—and never made it back to the hallowed ground of the World Series. His Yankee teams from his second tenure in New York were generally mediocre, his Detroit Tigers teams were mired in a severe rebuilding plan after the glory years of Al Kaline and Norm Cash, and his Boston Red Sox lacked the pitching and defense needed to win in the early 1980s.

As it was, Houk's two world championships put him into an elite class of managers. He remains one of a handful of skippers with two titles who are not members of the Hall of Fame; the others are the long-retired Bill Carrigan, Tom Kelly and Danny Murtaugh, and three more recent managers—Terry Francona, Cito Gaston, and Tony LaRussa—who will one day be eligible for Cooperstown. That is good company for Houk to keep. Murtaugh deserves to be in the Hall of Fame, LaRussa will make it one day, and strong arguments can be made in favor of Francona and Gaston. One can be made for Houk, too.

Wins and losses put aside, Houk left behind an indelible mark as an American hero. A veteran of World War II, Houk led his Ranger battalion during the Battle of the Bulge, an effort that earned him a Purple Heart and a Bronze Star. His wartime record earned him the label of "The Major," a nickname that matched his military rank during the war. Not surprisingly, he brought a level of discipline and respect from the battlefield to the ballfield. On three different occasions, Houk engaged in physical confrontations with sportswriters whom he felt had criticized him or his team without just cause. A tough guy through and through, Houk simply would not remain quiet if he felt his players were being treated unfairly.

Houk was a players' manager who exhibited patience to the extreme. He sometimes showed too much patience, allowing players like Bobby Richardson and Horace Clarke to bat in the leadoff position well after they had proven they could not. (In fairness to Houk, he managed before the sabermetric movement took hold, with its heavy emphasis on the importance of on-base percentage.) On the other hand, Houk nurtured an array of personalities from the raucous Mickey Mantle to the studious Tony Kubek, increased Whitey Ford's workload by allowing him to pitch every fourth day, and developed young talents like Thurman Munson, Bobby Murcer, and Roy White, who became building blocks for a new decade.

Ralph Houk remains underrated to this day. Because of the passing of time, many have forgotten about him. But those who followed the game in the 1960s and seventies know what an accomplished manager he was.

The King

Clyde King died just two days before Sparky Anderson did in November of 2010. It's safe to say that King's passing did not produce the same kind of back page headlines as the death of Anderson, a legend among managers and the owner of three world championship rings. But the death of King struck a chord with Yankee fans from the 1980s who remember how he restored some sanity to the frenetic whirlwind that enveloped the franchise that decade.

A lifelong baseball man, King came up as a pitcher with the Brooklyn Dodgers, where he became friends with Jackie Robinson. After his playing days, he managed the San Francisco Giants and Atlanta Braves, giving him the rare opportunity to manage both Willie Mays and Hank Aaron. In 1976, King moved onto the Yankees, as George Steinbrenner hired him to work in the front office. "The Boss" quickly took a liking to the affable and studious King, who impressed the owner with his knowledge of pitching. Critics of King knocked him for being The Boss' yes-man, and for allegedly serving as the owner's in-house spy, but he willingly took on any task assigned him, working as an advisor, super scout, pitching coach, and eventually as a manager and general manager.

King did his best work for the Yankees when he was given the most authority. That came in the middle of the 1984 season, when Steinbrenner fired the overmatched Murray Cook and made King the general manager. It didn't take long for King to start putting his imprint on the Yankees. Shortly after becoming GM, King traded an aging Roy Smalley to the Chicago White Sox for a player to be named later, who turned out to be future ace Doug Drabek.

The Yankees finished the 1984 season with 87 wins, but King recognized that the team needed a makeover, from the offense to the catching to the bench to the bullpen. As he prepared for the winter meetings in Houston, King developed a systematic plan of attack to rebuild the franchise. On the first day of the meetings, King acquired platoon catcher Ron Hassey and backup outfielder Henry Cotto from the Chicago Cubs for two spare parts, backup outfielder Brian Dayett and soft-tossing left-hander Ray Fontenot. Hassey would give the Yankees a strong, left-handed hitting catcher, while Cotto's speed and defense would serve him well as a fifth outfielder.

On the second day of the winter meetings, King made huge headlines when he put the finishing touches on a deal for the best leadoff man in history, Rickey Henderson. The trade cost the Yankees a young right-handed ace in Jose Rijo, but it also gave them a dynamic presence at the top of the lineup who could set the table for Don Mattingly and Dave Winfield. That same day, King stole hard-throwing right-hander Brian Fisher from the Atlanta Braves, giving up only journeyman catcher Rick Cerone in return. Fisher would become an imposing set-up man in front of closer Dave Righetti.

Not satisfied with his haul at the Houston meetings, King continued to do quietly good work that winter. He dumped two over-the-hill veterans, Steve Kemp and Tim Foli, sending them to the Pittsburgh Pirates for a young Jay Buhner. Except for the Buhner deal, which was made with the long term in mind, every one of King's trades would benefit the Yankees immediately in

1985. With their offense and bullpen improved, the Yankees won 97 games, a strong second behind the powerhouse Toronto Blue Jays.

King took a less aggressive approach during the winter of 1986-87, while sticking to his plan to promote young talent like Drabek, Dennis Rasmussen, Bob Tewksbury, and slugger Dan Pasqua. King's plan drew approval from the New York media. As the 1986 season progressed, Steinbrenner grew jealous of the accolades being sent King's way. The Boss became more meddlesome, putting pressure on King to make moves he did not want to make. Growing tired of Steinbrenner's interference, King stepped aside at the end of a 90-win season and return to the peaceful existence of a front office advisor.

If King had remained in power, it's possible that the Yankees would never have traded Buhner, Drabek, Tewksbury, and other promising youngsters for fading veterans. With King in control, the Yankees might have avoided the embarrassments of 1989 and 1990, when the franchise became a laughingstock.

As it turned out, King lost out on his chance for fame and glory, and made the transition into relative obscurity. That didn't seem to bother King, who didn't mind being in the background. All along, King remained one of the game's great storytellers. Always recognizable in his trademark horn-rimmed glasses, he loved to talk baseball, never turning down requests for interviews, and endlessly spinning his tales in his friendly southern drawl.

Clyde King was a baseball lifer, a man whose career lasted over six decades, and he loved every minute of it. And the Yankees of the mid-1980s were the better for it.

Matty Alou

A member of one of baseball's most famous families, Matty Alou, passed away in November of 2011 at the age of 72, leaving behind a legacy that included a brief but distinguished tenure in New York. Though he only played part of one season with the Yankees, he certainly left an impression on the franchise. Upon learning of his death, the Yankee organization officially remembered Alou with a written public tribute. Alou also left Yankee fans with an array of distinct memories, from his hitting to his distinct lack of size.

Alou became an intriguing player to follow because of an unconventional hitting style that seemed to break all the rules of batting. Alou swung a heavy bat, often hit off his front foot, and blooped a ton of singles to the opposite field, all of which made him fun to watch. Featuring an aggressive style and rarely showing interest in taking walks, Alou tended to swing at anything close to the strike zone. Ted Williams, perhaps the most cerebral and scientific hitter in history, could never figure out how Alou was successful. But the Dominican native could lace singles with the best of them. Alou batted for a high average, which coupled with his basestealing ability and the speed that allowed him to go from first to third, made him a useful player.

Alou began his career with the San Francisco Giants, where he had the unusual opportunity to play in the same outfield with his older brother, Felipe, and his younger brother, Jesus. But Matty never found much traction with the Giants. It was not until he was traded to the Pittsburgh Pirates, where he worked with a new manager in Harry "The Hat" Walker, that he became a star. The Hat completely retooled Alou's hitting approach, and to his credit, Alou accepted the advice like an eager student.

The results were astonishing. In 1966, Alou batted .342 to lead the National League. In his next three seasons, he batted

.338, .332, and .331. Alou also played a very good center field, showing range and a plus arm, making him a nearly complete package for the Pirates. All that Matty lacked was power.

By the time that Alou joined the Yankees in 1973, he was no longer the same player. Injuries robbed him of his arm strength, while slowing bat speed erased his abilities as a .330 hitter. But the Yankees felt he could help fill a void in right field, where everyone from Ron Woods to Johnny Callison had failed. The Yankees were set in the other outfield spots with reliable Roy White in left field and a young star like Bobby Murcer in center, but right field remained a problem. Alou stabilized the position, though he lacked the arm that one expects from a right fielder.

Though Alou played mostly in the outfield for the Yankees, he also made 40 appearances at first base. At five feet, nine inches, Alou looked odd playing a position that usually requires above-average height; he could have used a phone book to stand on first base and corral high throws from Horace Clarke, Gene "Stick" Michael, and Graig Nettles.

Strangely, the Yankees did not use Alou as a leadoff man, where he would have fit best. Instead, they batted him third, where his lack of power became more noticeable. But Alou hit well for the Yankees, batting .296 with an on-base percentage of nearly .340. If the Yankees had remained in contention in 1973, Alou would have lasted the entire season in New York. But the Yankees fell out of the pennant race, convincing them to try a late-season youth movement sans the Alou brothers. So on the same day, they sold Felipe Alou on waivers to the Montreal Expos and sent 34-year-old Matty to the St. Louis Cardinals, ridding themselves of two expensive contracts in the process.

As it turned out, Alou did not have much left in his hitting tank. He batted only .198 for the San Diego Padres in 1974, but did not want to leave the game. So he headed to Japan, where he put in three full seasons before finally retiring.

Alou was still playing in the Far East by the time the Yankees returned to championship status and won back-to-pennants in

1976 and '77. As with so many favorite old players from the 1960s and early seventies, like Jim Ray Hart, Bob Oliver, and Walt "No Neck" Williams, he did not last long enough to see the glory years in pinstripes.

But at the very least, fun players like Matty Alou made those lean years of the early 1970s a little more bearable for Yankee fans who grew up in that era. Those fans will always be grateful to players like Matty Alou.

BIBLIOGRAPHY

Berger, Phil. (1998). *Mickey Mantle: Biography.* Random House Value Publishing, Inc.

Berra, Lawrence Peter, & Horton, Thomas N. (1989). *Yogi: It Ain't Over.* McGraw-Hill Publishing Company.

Bouton, Jim. (1970). *Ball Four: My Life and Hard Times Throwing The Knuckleball in the Big Leagues.* The World Publishing Company.

Creamer, Robert W. (1974). *Babe: The Legend Comes to Life.* Simon and Schuster.

Frommer, Harvey. (1997). *The New York Yankee Encyclopedia.* Simon & Schuster Macmillan Company.

Gallico, Paul. (1942). *Lou Gehrig: Pride of the Yankees.* Grosset & Dunlap.

Nettles, Graig, & Golenbock, Peter. (1984). *Balls* G.P. Putnam's Sons.

Piniella, Lou, & Allen, Maury. (1986). *Sweet Lou.* Bantam Books.

Winfield, Dave with Parker, Tom. (1988). *Winfield: A Player's Life.* W.W. Norton & Company.